A clinician's brief guide to the Mental Capacity Act

A clinician's brief guide to the Mental Capacity Act

Second edition

Nick Brindle, Tim Branton, Alison Stansfield and Tony Zigmond

RCPsych Publications

First edition © The Royal College of Psychiatrists 2013
Second edition © The Royal College of Psychiatrists 2015

RCPsych Publications is an imprint of the Royal College of Psychiatrists,
21 Prescot Street, London E1 8BB
http://www.rcpsych.ac.uk

British Library Cataloguing-in-Publication Data.
A catalogue record for this book is available from the British Library.
ISBN 978-1-909726-42-0

Distributed in North America by Publishers Storage and Shipping Company.

Printed by Bell & Bain Limited, Glasgow, UK

Contents

Preface

Although this is a partner volume to *A Clinician's Brief Guide to the Mental Health Act,*[1] the Mental Health Act and the Mental Capacity Act are very different in both their scope (the Mental Capacity Act being much more widely relevant) and provisions. The authority of the Mental Capacity Act is frequently used without the user realising it. For clinicians, it has largely replaced the common law as the authority for providing medical care and treatment to people (over 16 years of age) who lack the capacity to consent for themselves.

This book is designed as an easy-to-read and interesting guide to understanding those parts of the Mental Capacity Act 2005 (MCA), including the 2007 Deprivation of Liberty amendments, which clinicians need in their daily practice. It covers how to assess whether a person lacks capacity; the range, scope and limitations of the various authorities to treat, including 'best interests' decisions, advance decisions and lasting powers of attorney; and the range of safeguards in place, such as the Deprivation of Liberty Safeguards (DoLs), the Court of Protection and Independent Mental Health Advocates. It also includes relevant aspects of the Human Rights Act 1998, the Mental Health Act 1983 and illustrative case law. Although it should be of particular interest to clinicians in England and Wales, it will aid the understanding of everyone who helps care for people who cannot make decisions for themselves or who wishes to make legal provision for their own future care.

More detailed guidance can be found in the Mental Capacity Act and Deprivation of Liberty Safeguards Codes of Practice[2,3] and many other texts. Acts of Parliament and secondary legislation such as Statutory Instruments can be read and downloaded from the internet. These are readily searchable electronically, so to avoid cluttering the text with numbers we have not cited chapter and verse when using short quotations from Acts.

Acronyms and abbreviations abound in this legislation. We have used very few of these, but readers may find those listed on p. vii useful when reading other sources.

The MCA throughout refers to 'P' and the DoLS provisions to the 'relevant person'. As clinicians, we will refer to individuals as people or patients, depending on which seems the most appropriate.

It should be noted that the Mental Capacity Act and its accompanying Codes of Practice (one for the main part of the Act, another for the Deprivation of Liberty Safeguards) apply in England and Wales but not elsewhere in the UK. The Mental Health Act, however, has distinct codes for the two jurisdictions.

Preface to the second edition

Compared with the Mental Health Act, the Mental Capacity Act is newer, the scope so much wider and, consequently, the case law remains in a relatively accelerated state of evolution. The output from the Court of Protection has been copious and two important cases relating to the Mental Capacity Act have come before the Supreme Court. In this second edition we have therefore included more in the way of clinically relevant issues that have emerged from the courts since first publication in order to bridge the gap between court judgments and the practising clinician.

The main topics that have been updated in this edition are:

▶ the interface between the Mental Health Act and the Mental Capacity Act, identifying the appropriate legal authority to use in clinical decision-making and clarifying the margins of the doctrine of necessity

▶ the Supreme Court judgment in relation to 'Cheshire West', how this affects the threshold of what is considered deprivation of liberty and the implications of the judgment on health and social care practice

▶ assessment of capacity and clarifying the threshold of decision-making incapacity

▶ the guidance for clinicians who may become involved in Court of Protection proceedings, which we have expanded and clarified with explanation of specific areas of clinically relevant case law.

Common abbreviations and terms

AC   Approved Clinician
AMHP   Approved Mental Health Professional
BIA   Best Interests Assessor
CQC   Care Quality Commission
CTO   Community Treatment Order
DoLS   Deprivation of Liberty Safeguards
ECHR   European Convention on Human Rights
ECtHR   European Court of Human Rights
HM   Hospital Manager
HRA   Human Rights Act 1998
IMCA   Independent Mental Capacity Advocate
IMHA   Independent Mental Health Advocate
LD   Learning Disability (i.e. intellectual disability)
MCA   Mental Capacity Act 2005
MHA   Mental Health Act 1983
ND   Nominated Deputy
NR   Nearest Relative
RC   Responsible Clinician
RMP   Registered Medical Practitioner

The legal framework: the Mental Capacity Act, the Human Rights Act and common law

Clinical practice involves doing things to, and for, other people. Touching, undressing, examining and medicating another person require some legal authority. Depending on the circumstances, that authority is established in England and Wales within the common law, the Mental Capacity Act 2005 (MCA), the Mental Health Act 1983 (MHA) and, underpinning it all, the European Convention on Human Rights (ECHR) as incorporated into the Human Rights Act 1998.

▶ **Common law** is judge-made law. It is a body of law made up entirely of principles developed organically from individual court cases on a case-by-case basis. As Lord Donaldson said, 'The common law is common sense under a wig'.[4] Common law cannot be used where there is a statutory alternative, i.e. statute law overrides common law. For those practitioners who worked prior to 2005, this is particularly important. The common law authority to act in the best interests of a person who lacks capacity has been almost entirely replaced by the MCA.

▶ **Statute laws** are laws passed by Parliament and called Acts.

▶ **Judicial interpretation of statute law** Judges also interpret the statutes passed by Parliament and make rulings on these.

▶ **European Law** is a potentially confusing term because there are two distinct types of European law. There is European Law passed by the European Union (EU). These laws tend to make specific requirements of member countries and are binding on those countries. An example is the European Working Time Directive. The other European law, and in relation to clinical decision-making much more relevant, is the European Convention on Human Rights (ECHR). This is incorporated into UK law by the Human Rights Act 1998. The latter makes some specific requirements of UK national laws (which must be compatible with the ECHR) and also sets a framework for the interpretation of national laws and practices both by the UK courts and individual clinicians.

▶ **State compliance with the ECHR** is determined by the European Court of Human Rights (ECtHR).

▶ **In relation to consent to medical treatment**, unless a patient is subject to the Mental Health Act, the common law and statutory criminal law determine the rules for clinicians whose patients have decision-making capacity. For patients who lack capacity, the Mental Capacity Act gives the legal framework (the only exception to this is when a person who lacks capacity needs control or restraint in the interests of someone else, e.g. to prevent them hurting another person). That is, the MCA provides a statutory framework for decision-making and the care and treatment of people who lack decision-making capacity. It also introduced substitute decision-making powers in the form of advance refusals of medical treatment, lasting powers of attorney and deputies appointed by the Court of Protection (Court Appointed Deputies). The Act provides safeguards in the form of a new Court of Protection, the Office of the Public Guardian, the Independent Mental Capacity Advocate and a new criminal offence of ill-treating or neglecting a person lacking capacity.

The MCA is underpinned by five key principles:

▶ **a presumption of capacity** – every adult has the right to make their own decisions and must be assumed to have capacity to do so unless it is proved otherwise

▶ **support in decision-making** – a person must be given all practicable help before anyone treats them as not being able to make their own decisions

▶ **acceptance of unwise decisions** – just because an individual makes what might be seen as an unwise decision, they should not be treated as lacking capacity to make that decision

▶ **acting in the best interests** – an act done or decision made under the Act for or on behalf of a person who lacks capacity must be done in their best interests

▶ **taking the least restrictive option** – anything done for or on behalf of a person who lacks capacity should be the least restrictive of their basic rights and freedoms.

The main provisions of the MCA are:

▶ **A definition of incapacity** The Act introduced a test for incapacity. First, there must be evidence of an impairment of, or disturbance in the functioning of, the mind or brain. Second, the person must be unable to make a decision because of that impairment or disturbance. The test is decision- and time-specific.

▶ **Best interests** The Act requires that all decisions in relation to a person lacking capacity must be in their best interests. Decision makers must work through a checklist to establish best interests.

▶ **Acts in connection with care and treatment** The Act gives a clear legal authority, and protection, for those who make decisions on behalf of, or care for, people who lack capacity in relation to the matter in question, so long as they act in that person's best interests.

- **Restraint** The Act defines restraint as the use of force or the threat of use of force. Restraint is only authorised for the prevention of harm to the person themselves and must be proportionate to the likelihood and seriousness of the harm.

- **Deprivation of liberty** The Act includes a schedule to provide authorisation for depriving a person who lacks capacity of their liberty, so long as it is in the best interests of that person and there are no less restrictive alternatives.

- **Lasting powers of attorney (LPAs)** The person can decide whether to have one or several attorneys (also called donees); if several, how they should act together; and whether they can make decisions regarding property and affairs, or health and welfare, or both.

- **Court Appointed Deputies** The Act gives the Court of Protection the authority to appoint deputies to take decisions on health, welfare and/ or financial matters as authorised by the Court.

- **Advance decisions to refuse treatment** The Act allows people to make anticipatory decisions – decisions in advance of losing capacity – to refuse medical treatment should they lack capacity in the future. The Act sets safeguards in relation to advance decisions. Decisions must be both applicable and valid. If the decision relates to the withholding or withdrawing of life-sustaining treatment there are additional requirements.

- **Independent Mental Capacity Advocates (IMCAs)** The Act requires the involvement of an Independent Mental Capacity Advocate in specified circumstances. When the decision relates to serious medical treatment or a change in the accommodation of a person who lacks capacity, and the person has no family member or friend to speak for them, an Independent Mental Capacity Advocate must be appointed.

- **Research** The Act sets out the conditions and requirements governing research involving people who lack capacity.

- **A criminal offence** A person found guilty of ill treatment or neglect of a person who lacks capacity may be liable to imprisonment for a term of up to 5 years.

A number of matters fall outside the scope of the MCA:

- marriage/civil partnerships
- divorce
- sexual relationships
- placing a child for adoption
- taking over parental responsibility for a child
- consent to fertility treatment
- voting
- detention/treatment of people under the authority of the Mental Health Act.

Age and the Mental Capacity Act

The MCA applies to people aged 16 and over, with the following exceptions:

▶ Under the age of 16:

  ▶ if the child is unable to make decisions about property or finances and is unlikely to acquire capacity when they reach 18, then the Court of Protection can make the decision or appoint a deputy to do so (section 18(3))

  ▶ offences of ill-treatment or wilful neglect of a person who lacks capacity (section 2(1)) includes child victims (section 44).

▶ Under the age of 18 a person cannot:

  ▶ make a lasting power of attorney

  ▶ make an advance decision to refuse medical treatment

  ▶ apply to the Court of Protection.

Note

There are some overlaps in legislation. The Code of Practice refers to 'children' as people under the age of 16 and 'young people' as people aged 16–17, whereas in the Children Act 1989 and the law more generally the term 'child' refers to people under 18.

Note

The term 'learning disability' is used throughout this book. We recognise that many clinicians, and others, are more familiar with or prefer the term 'intellectual disability'. We are using learning disability because it is the term used and defined in the MHA ('a state of arrested or incomplete development of the mind which includes significant impairment of intelligence and social functioning') and used throughout the secondary legislation and Codes of Practice.

An individual carrying out care or treatment of a young person aged 16–17 who lacks capacity to consent will generally have protection from liability provided that they follow the principles of the Act. When assessing best interests, the individual providing care or treatment must consult others involved in the person's care or welfare if it is practical and appropriate to do so, and this may include parents. It is important that in such circumstances, care is taken not to unlawfully breach the young person's rights to confidentiality.

If there is disagreement about the care, treatment or welfare of a young person who lacks capacity to make relevant decisions, then, depending on the circumstances, the case may be heard in the family courts or the Court of Protection. Cases may be transferred between the Court of Protection and the family courts, depending on what is appropriate for the particular circumstances. For example, if there is a parental dispute about the best place of residence for a 17-year-old with severe learning (i.e. intellectual) disability, it may be appropriate for the Court of Protection to deal with the disputed issues, because orders made under the Children Act 1989 will expire when the young person becomes 18.

European law and the Human Rights Act

Understanding European institutions isn't easy or, thankfully, necessary here. Our concern is with the European Convention on Human Rights. This was adopted by the Council of Europe (a group of 42 States) in 1951. The UK was one of the first signatories to the Convention. Although before 2000, when the Human Rights Act 1998 came into force, 'public authorities' (the term used to describe 'the State') and private institutions providing public functions were supposedly obliged to comply with the Convention, it was difficult in practice for an aggrieved person to obtain a judgment because they needed to exhaust all domestic legal remedies before they could appeal to the European Court of Human Rights. The Human Rights Act changed this. Parliament is required to ensure that its laws are compliant with the European Convention on Human Rights, and courts and other public authorities are required to interpret Acts in line with the Convention as far as possible. European Court of Human Rights judgments are applicable (although not binding) in UK courts.

The Human Rights Act 1998

The Human Rights Act incorporated the European Convention on Human Rights into UK law. In clinical practice, references to the Human Rights Act and to the European Convention on Human Rights are interchangeable. The purpose of the Convention is to ensure that governments behave with a proper regard for human rights (it followed the atrocities of the Second World War). It does not apply directly to private companies or citizens unless they are carrying out public functions in the place of the government. It is for governments to legislate to make private bodies and citizens behave properly. It is unlawful for a public authority (the government or its agents) to act incompatibly with the European Convention on Human Rights. If they do, the Convention allows for a case to be brought in a UK court. Clinicians, when treating a National Health Service (NHS) patient or a private patient on behalf of the State, act as public authorities. They do not do so when treating paying private patients. Private hospitals are public authorities when providing services to NHS-funded patients. Professionals must keep the European Convention on Human Rights in mind when conducting their clinical practice. The Articles of major relevance are the following (that's not to say the others are irrelevant):

▶ Article 2, the right to life
▶ Article 3, the prohibition of torture and inhuman and degrading treatment
▶ Article 5, the right to liberty and security
▶ Article 6, the right to a fair trial
▶ Article 8, the right to respect for private and family life.

The European Convention on Human Rights requires all UK legislation to be interpreted, as far as possible, in accordance with Convention rights. If a UK court decides that it cannot interpret an Act in a way that is compatible with the Convention, it has to make a 'declaration of incompatibility' (between UK law and the European Convention on Human Rights) so that the government can ask Parliament to change the law. This does not override Parliament. The Act remains unaltered until amended by Parliament. Parliament has a fast-track method for amending Acts under such circumstances.

The European Convention on Human Rights is said to be a 'living' document. It is expected that the way courts interpret its Articles will change over time, developing in line with the current mores of society. There are three categories of rights under the Convention:

▶ 'absolute' – no excuses (e.g. Article 3)
▶ 'limited' – there are specific, explicit circumstances, defined in the Article, when it doesn't apply (e.g. Article 5)
▶ 'qualified' – interference is permitted in a range of circumstances (e.g. Article 8).

One potential difficulty is that one person's rights may compete with another person's. For example, should there be an absolute right to practise one's religion? Clearly not, if to do so involves sacrificing the lives or freedoms of others. Furthermore, some Articles appear to clash and a balance must be struck. For example, Article 2, which puts a positive duty on the State to preserve life, may conflict with Article 8, which requires the State not to interfere in people's lives. Indeed, there may be a problem even within a single Article. Should, for example, a person with a learning disability who cannot make these decisions for themselves be left with their family (assuming that is the family's wish), or be moved to encourage living an independent life (against the family's wish)? Article 8 is respect for both family and private life and has been used by both sides in support of their argument.

One of the most useful concepts introduced by the European Convention on Human Rights is that of 'proportionality'. This says that any interference with a Convention right must be proportionate to the intended aims and the aims themselves must be legitimate. How much force can be used in a particular circumstance, for example an interference with a person's physical integrity, depends on the severity of the threat to the person or to others.

Finally, it is perhaps worth noting that only a public authority, including private bodies when exercising public functions, can be sued under the Human Rights Act and only victims can sue. Identifying the victim may not always be obvious. A patient's daughter successfully sued a hospital when her mother, while detained under the MHA, died by suicide (the hospital had breached Article 2, the patient's right to life, by providing care that was not of the required standard).[5]

The following section looks at specific human rights legislation. In an attempt to limit confusion, only the most relevant Articles are reproduced and discussed.

Convention Articles

Article 2: Right to life

1. Everyone's right to life shall be protected by law. No one shall be deprived of his life intentionally save in the execution of a sentence of a court following his conviction of a crime for which this penalty is provided by law.
2. Deprivation of life shall not be regarded as inflicted in contravention of this article when it results from the use of force which is no more than absolutely necessary:
   a. in defence of any person from unlawful violence;
   b. in order to effect a lawful arrest or to prevent escape of a person lawfully detained;
   c. in action lawfully taken for the purpose of quelling a riot or insurrection.

Article 2 puts a positive duty on the State. An institution will not have breached Article 2 if it has done everything correctly but there is poor practice or negligence by an individual member of staff. Article 2 also covers the clinician's duty to pass on sensitive information about serious risks to others when transferring the care of a mentally disordered patient, including the need to consider the risks to other in-patients (e.g. ensuring an appropriate environment if admitting a very disturbed patient). Other examples include: 'do not attempt cardiopulmonary resuscitation' (DNACPR) orders, withdrawal of life-sustaining/prolonging treatments, and arguments about when the State will not fund particular treatments. An interesting example arose in a case concerning conjoined twins. Separating the twins would result in the immediate death of one twin, but not separating them would lead to the death of both. It was argued that one of the twins was interfering in the right to life of the other.[6]

The State's responsibilities are greater in relation to those who are in its custody, such as prisoners. Patients detained under the MHA or the

Deprivation of Liberty Safeguards of the MCA come under this category. Additionally, the right to life and the obligations it puts on clinicians apply at an enhanced level to psychiatric patients, even those admitted informally (voluntarily). As Lady Hale, one of the judges in the case of Rabone[7] explained, voluntary psychiatric patients who have consented to admission to hospital (such as Ms Rabone) may not be in the same position as physically ill patients who have consented, because the former (a) may have impaired capacity, (b) may be consenting because they fear detention and (c) can be detained under section 5 of the MHA.

Article 3: Prohibition of torture and inhuman and degrading treatment

No one shall be subjected to torture or to inhuman or degrading treatment or punishment.

Article 3 is an absolute right. A person can argue that their care and/or treatment is incompatible with Article 3 and its protection of fundamental human dignity without having to point to (or be capable of pointing to) any specific ill-effects arising from it. For example, tying an elderly patient to a bed may breach Article 3 even though the patient isn't physically harmed. Equally, neglect of a person that leads to death may be a breach of Article 3 rather than Article 2. The threshold for Article 3 is high. In the case of *Herczegfalvy v Austria*,[8] a patient complained that he had been forcibly administered food and antipsychotics, isolated and attached to a security bed with handcuffs. The European Court of Human Rights held that 'as a general rule a measure which is a therapeutic necessity cannot be regarded as inhuman or degrading'. The medical intervention must, of course, be 'a necessity'. As was pointed out by Lady Hale, the judge in a case from Broadmoor hospital, 'Forcible measures inflicted upon an incapacitated patient which are not a medical necessity may indeed be inhuman or degrading'.[9]

Furthermore, the UK has breached Article 3, for example in the case of a man taken to a police station under section 136 of the MHA. He was kept in a cell for four days although he was clearly seriously mentally ill: shouting, taking off all his clothes, banging his head on the wall, drinking from the toilet and smearing himself with food and faeces. The European Court of Human Rights said 'Even though there was no intention to humiliate or debase him, the Court finds that the conditions which the applicant was required to endure were an affront to human dignity and reached the threshold of degrading treatment for the purposes of Article 3'.[10]

Article 5: Right to liberty and security of person

1. Everyone has the right to liberty and security of person. No one shall be deprived of his liberty save in the following cases and in accordance with a procedure prescribed by law:
   a. the lawful detention of a person after conviction by a competent court;
   b. the lawful arrest or detention of a person for non-compliance with the lawful order of a court or in order to secure the fulfilment of any obligation prescribed by law;
   c. the lawful arrest or detention of a person effected for the purpose of bringing him before the competent legal authority on reasonable suspicion of having committed an offence or when it is reasonably considered necessary to prevent his committing an offence or fleeing after having done so;
   d. the detention of a minor by lawful order for the purpose of educational supervision or his lawful detention for the purpose of bringing him before the competent legal authority;
   e. the lawful detention of persons for the prevention of the spreading of infectious diseases, of persons of unsound mind, alcoholics or drug addicts, or vagrants;
   f. the lawful arrest or detention of a person to prevent his effecting an unauthorised entry into the country or of a person against whom action is being taken with a view to deportation or extradition.
2. Everyone who is arrested shall be informed promptly, in a language which he understands, of the reasons for his arrest and of any charge against him.
3. Everyone arrested or detained in accordance with the provisions of paragraph 1c. of this Article shall be brought promptly before a judge or other officer authorised by law to exercise judicial power and shall be entitled to trial within a reasonable time or to release pending trial. Release may be conditioned by guarantees to appear for trial.
4. Everyone who is deprived of his liberty by arrest or detention shall be entitled to take proceedings by which the lawfulness of his detention shall be decided speedily by a court and his release ordered if the detention is not lawful.
5. Everyone who has been the victim of arrest or detention in contravention of the provisions of this Article shall have an enforceable right to compensation.

Article 5 is central to issues relating to the Deprivation of Liberty Safeguards (DoLS) of the MCA (discussed in Chapter 7) and the MHA. Paragraph 1(e) of Article 5 allows for 'the lawful detention of persons for the prevention of the spreading of infectious diseases, of persons of unsound mind, alcoholics or drug addicts, or vagrants'. What is meant by unsound mind and who decides that a person is so suffering? In a pivotal case, *Winterwerp v The Netherlands*,[11] the European Court of Human Rights said:

'A person cannot be detained as being of unsound mind unless he or she is reliably shown to be so as demonstrated by objective medical expertise and the nature or degree of his or her mental disorder is such as to justify the deprivation of liberty. The detention ceases to be valid when the relevant mental disorder disappears or ceases to be such as justifies the deprivation of liberty.'

This is important because it means that a detained patient's mental state must be kept under constant review by the clinician responsible for their care and the patient must be discharged from detention under the MHA, or MCA Deprivation of Liberty Safeguards, if they are deemed no longer to be suffering from any mental disorder.

Article 6: Right to a fair trial

1. In the determination of his civil rights and obligations or of any criminal charge against him, everyone is entitled to a fair and public hearing within a reasonable time by an independent and impartial tribunal established by law. Judgment shall be pronounced publicly but the press and public may be excluded from all or part of the trial in the interest of morals, public order or national security in a democratic society, where the interests of juveniles or the protection of the private life of the parties so require, or to the extent strictly necessary in the opinion of the court in special circumstances where publicity would prejudice the interests of justice.
2. Everyone charged with a criminal offence shall be presumed innocent until proved guilty according to law.
3. Everyone charged with a criminal offence has the following minimum rights:
   a. to be informed promptly, in a language which he understands and in detail, of the nature and cause of the accusation against him;
   b. to have adequate time and facilities for the preparation of his defence;
   c. to defend himself in person or through legal assistance of his own choosing or, if he has not sufficient means to pay for legal assistance, to be given it free when the interests of justice so require;
   d. to examine or have examined witnesses against him and to obtain the attendance and examination of witnesses on his behalf under the same conditions as witnesses against him;
   e. to have the free assistance of an interpreter if he cannot understand or speak the language used in court.

Article 6 is important not only in relation to civil and criminal cases but also, for example, in tribunals (e.g. disability, employment, mental health), General Medical Council and other professional body hearings, and employment and disciplinary procedures.

Article 8: Right to respect for private and family life

1. Everyone has the right to respect for his private and family life, his home and his correspondence.
2. There shall be no interference by a public authority with the exercise of this right except such as is in accordance with the law and is necessary in a democratic society in the interests of national security, public safety or the economic well-being of the country, for the prevention of disorder or crime, for the protection of health or morals, or for the protection of the rights and freedoms of others.

The notion of private life in Article 8 is broad and covers an individual's right to personal autonomy and to physical integrity. Doing anything to a person's body, such as giving a medicine or injection without consent, is a potential Article 8 breach. It is a qualified right. It can be overridden, if necessary, on the grounds given. Consequently, patient confidentiality can be overridden in certain circumstances (e.g. in informing the Driver and Vehicle Licensing Agency about a patient who may be unfit to drive, or informing the police about a patient who may pose a danger to others). In such situations, the patient's consent to release information should always be sought, if possible. Article 8 was used in a case arguing that it was unlawful to ban smoking in hospitals that are effectively patients' homes and that the patients cannot leave (the maximum-security hospitals). The court decided that the exceptions within Article 8 were met and upheld the smoking ban.[12] Seclusion, restraint, strip-searching, access to medical records, family visiting rights, same-sex accommodation and so on are all issues that come within the bounds of Article 8. Indeed, 'even a minor interference with the physical integrity of an individual must be regarded as an interference with the right to respect for private life under Article 8 if it is carried out against the individual's will'.[13]

Article 9: Freedom of thought, conscience and religion

1. Everyone has the right to freedom of thought, conscience and religion; this right includes freedom to change his religion or belief and freedom, either alone or in community with others and in public or private, to manifest his religion or belief, in worship, teaching, practice and observance.
2. Freedom to manifest one's religion or beliefs shall be subject only to such limitations as are prescribed by law and are necessary in a democratic society in the interests of public safety, for the protection of public order, health or morals, or for the protection of the rights and freedoms of others.

Article 12: Right to marry

Men and women of marriageable age have the right to marry and to found a family, according to the national laws governing the exercise of this right.

Article 13: Right to an effective remedy

Everyone whose rights and freedoms as set forth in this Convention are violated shall have an effective remedy before a national authority notwithstanding that the violation has been committed by persons acting in an official capacity.

In relation to Article 13, compensation has, for example, been paid to patients when their Tribunal hearing has been significantly delayed and to the family of a detained patient whose right to life was violated when poor standards enabled her to take her own life.[5]

Article 14: Prohibition of discrimination

The enjoyment of the rights and freedoms set forth in this Convention shall be secured without discrimination on any ground such as sex, race, colour, language, religion, political or other opinion, national or social origin, association with a national minority, property, birth or other status.

Article 14 does not give a free-standing right to non-discrimination but requires the exercise of the other rights to be carried out in a non-discriminatory way. So if there is a distinction between the way people with mental disorder are treated compared with the treatment of those with a physical disorder, the Article might apply.

The UK is also a signatory to other important international conventions, including the United Nations Convention on the Rights of Persons with Disabilities (2008) and the United Nations Convention on the Rights of the Child (1989). Although both conventions have been ratified, neither has been incorporated into UK law.

Common law

Consent to medical treatment – adults

Clinicians are familiar with seeking and obtaining consent for treatment from patients. If the patient has the capacity to make the required decision(s), then the patient is the legal authority for the clinician to proceed with treatment. The validity of that authority depends on whether the practitioner has established consent within the framework of common law and documented it appropriately. So proper consent to treatment protects both the patient from treatment they do not want and the clinician from liability for wrongdoing. The MHA Code of Practice defines consent as:

> '[the] voluntary and continuing permission of a patient to be given a particular treatment, based on a sufficient knowledge of the purpose, nature, likely effects and risks of that treatment, including the likelihood of its success and any alternatives to it. Permission given under any unfair or undue pressure is not consent.'[14]

Consent may take different forms. It may be stated or implied but need not be expressly declared or written for it to be legally valid. For example, a patient holding out their arm for a clinician to measure their blood pressure may imply consent to this investigation even if the patient cannot speak.

Understanding the principles that underpin consent by patients who are able to make decisions is essential for understanding the legal framework for those who lack capacity. The case law relating to consent to medical treatment follows two themes. The first is the right of the capacitous patient to refuse treatment and the second is defining the duty of the practitioner to provide appropriate information to help the patient in making the decision.

The principle of autonomy

Every human being of adult years and sound mind has a right to determine what shall be done with their own body. A clinician who performs an operation or other medical procedure on such a person without their consent is not merely negligent. This is trespass of the person (a tort or civil wrong for which damages may be liable) and an assault (i.e. a criminal act which may lead to a criminal conviction). This, of course, doesn't apply in an emergency if the patient is unable to consent and it is necessary to operate or carry out the procedure before consent can be obtained.

Lord Donaldson, considering a case in which clinicians sought authority to administer a blood transfusion to a patient who had refused a transfusion stated that 'Every adult has the right and capacity [*sic*] to decide whether or not he will accept medical treatment, even if a refusal may risk permanent injury to his health or even lead to premature death [...] it matters not whether the reason for the refusal were rational or irrational, unknown or even non-existent'.[15]

In another case, medical staff were required to switch off the patient's ventilator, leading to her death, because she had capacity and refused the treatment. Dame Butler-Sloss used almost identical words to Lord Donaldson, 'A competent patient has an absolute right to refuse to consent to medical treatment for any reason, rational or irrational, or for no reason at all, even when that decision may lead to his or her death'.[16]

In a recent case, the judge, Justice Jackson, could not have made the legal position clearer: 'The freedom to choose for oneself is a part of what it means to be a human being. For this reason, anyone capable of making decisions has an absolute right to accept or refuse medical treatment, regardless of the wisdom or consequences of the decision. The decision does not have to be justified to anyone. In the absence of consent any invasion of the body will be a criminal assault. The fact that the intervention is well-meaning or therapeutic makes no difference'.[17]

These judgments assert the principle of autonomy. The influence of these cases can be found in the principles of the MCA that recognise an assumption of capacity and the freedom to make unwise decisions. The judges' language is somewhat unhelpful, however, as an irrational refusal of medical treatment may constitute evidence of incapacity. Indeed, the apparently irrational refusal of medical treatment may alert a practitioner to a difficulty with decision-making capacity. This is not to suggest that the principle that people have a right to make unwise decisions is wrong or that making an unwise decision is synonymous with lack of capacity. The provisions of the MCA and its Code of Practice[2] may provide authority and guidance in these circumstances.

Providing information to patients

Bolam v Friern Hospital Management Committee[18] is a case familiar to most clinicians. The case concerned a patient who suffered a fracture of the hip during electroconvulsive therapy (ECT) conducted without a muscle relaxant or restraint. The standards of practice at issue in Bolam were not only anaesthetic practice and restraint in relation to ECT, but also the information given to the patient before the procedure. In relation to all these issues it was held that the practitioner had not been negligent as his practice had been in accordance with a responsible body of opinion (a legal construct subsequently known as the Bolam test), i.e. a group of clinicians acted in a way that would be thought reasonable practice by a group of their peers. While this test (what would a group of similar professionals do?) remains important, the decision does have to be capable of withstanding logical analysis and the judge is entitled to hold that the body of opinion is not reasonable or responsible.[19]

The responsibility of the clinician is to act in consideration of what information a 'reasonable patient' might expect. If a treatment carries a significant risk that might influence the decision of a reasonable patient, then in the normal course it is the responsibility of the clinician to inform the patient of that risk, so that the patient can determine for themselves whether or not to consent.[20]

The General Medical Council recognises that information-giving and consultation are central to the doctor–patient relationship and that the justification for medical paternalism is diminishing. It has issued detailed guidance for doctors, emphasising partnership between doctors and patients and participation in decisions about treatment.[21] The guidance proposes a basic model for establishing consent that includes the following steps:

▶ Assessment of the patient's condition.
▶ An explanation of the condition, the options available, the risks and benefits of each option, and the effect of no intervention, covering:
  ▶ the diagnosis and prognosis
  ▶ any uncertainties about the diagnosis or prognosis, including options for further investigations
  ▶ options for treating or managing the condition, including the option not to treat
  ▶ the purpose of any proposed investigation or treatment and what it will involve
  ▶ the potential benefits, risks and burdens, and the likelihood of success, for each option; this should include information, if available, about whether the benefits or risks are affected by which organisation or doctor is chosen to provide care

- ► whether a proposed investigation or treatment is part of a research programme or is an innovative treatment designed specifically for the patient's benefit
- ► the people who will be mainly responsible for and involved in the patient's care, what their roles are, and to what extent students may be involved
- ► the patient's right to refuse to take part in teaching or research
- ► the patient's right to seek a second opinion
- ► any bills the patient will have to pay
- ► any conflicts of interest that the clinician, or their organisation, may have
- ► any treatments that the clinician believes have greater potential benefit for the patient than those they or their organisation can offer.

► The patient weighs up the options and decides. A capacitous patient may refuse the intervention.

► If the patient chooses investigations or treatment that the clinician believes are inadvisable, the clinician is not obliged to provide them but should explore the reasons for the request, explain their position and consider referring for a second opinion.

► Clinicians need to tailor their decision-making approach to the patient, taking into account:

- ► the patient's needs, wishes and priorities
- ► their level of knowledge about, and understanding of, their condition
- ► their prognosis and the treatment options
- ► the nature of their condition
- ► the complexity of the treatment
- ► the nature and level of risk associated with the investigation or treatment.

Coercion and consent

In the case mentioned above (p. 13) of the patient who refused a blood transfusion, it was suggested that the patient's mother, a Jehovah's Witness, had exercised undue influence over her daughter's decision.[15] Lord Donaldson noted that the test in relation to duress is: 'Does the patient really mean what he says or is he merely saying it for a quiet life, to satisfy someone else or because the advice and persuasion to which he has been subjected is such that he can no longer think and decide for himself?'.[15]

Common law doctrine of necessity

For many years this was the authority clinicians used when treating patients who lacked the capacity to make treatment decisions for themselves. The MCA, in sections 5 and 6, has generally replaced the doctrine of necessity as the authority for treating patients who lack capacity. A judge in a case involving a man with severe autism who was restrained by the police clarified the legal position in the following way: 'For my part I am satisfied that where the provisions of the Mental Capacity Act apply, the common law defence of necessity has no application'.[23] For the sake of completeness it is also worth noting that in a different case the judge said 'Part II of the Mental Health Act 1983 provides a comprehensive code for compulsory admission to hospital for non-compliant incapacitated patients such as the Claimant. The common law principle of necessity does not apply in this context'.[24]

So when, if ever, is the common law doctrine of necessity still relevant? One might suggest that it is still applicable when a person who lacks capacity presents a risk solely to others, i.e. when the intervention cannot be said to be in that person's best interests because, under that circumstance, the intervention cannot be under the authority of the MCA.

Summary of common law in relation to consent for adults

Practitioners who can demonstrate that they have provided the appropriate information for a patient to make a decision and give consent to an investigation or treatment will not be found liable for trespass. The authority to investigate or treat comes from the patient.

It is worth mentioning that above the age of 18, age itself, in law, does not affect a person's ability to make a decision. It has been suggested that, in practice, older people (like those with disabilities) are sometimes treated as if they do not have mental capacity – solely on the basis of their age. To do so is, of course, wrong.

Consent to medical treatment – minors

The age of majority (that is the age at which the law recognises someone as an adult) has varied markedly over the centuries. It is currently 18 in the UK. This means that until the age of 18, young people (minors) may still be subject to the jurisdiction of the courts. Over the years, legislative and other changes, including European and UK case law, have made the subject of consent relating to minors very much more complex than that relating to adults. Only a brief outline is within the scope of this book.

Overarching all other legal provisions for minors is the Children Act 1989. Its provisions apply to all people under 18. It has been amended several times (most significantly by the Adoption and Children Act 2002, the Children Act 2004 and the Children and Adoption Act 2006), but the 1989 framework remains intact.[25] It established that the welfare of children is of paramount importance. It also introduced the concept of parental responsibility.

The Family Law Reform Act 1969 gave 16- and 17-year-olds the authority to consent to medical treatment:

> 'The consent of a minor who has attained the age of sixteen years to any surgical, medical or dental treatment [...] shall be as effective as it would be

if he were of full age; and where a minor has [...] given an effective consent to any treatment it shall not be necessary to obtain any consent for it from his parent or guardian.'

However, unlike with adults, the refusal of a competent 16- or 17-year-old could be overridden by either an individual with parental responsibility or a court.[22] This has changed since the introduction of the MCA. As with adults, the law now requires the presumption of capacity for anyone aged 16 and over, and so if a 16- or 17-year-old has capacity, they can consent to or refuse medical treatment. However, a 16- or 17-year-old may be unable to make a decision because 'they are overwhelmed by the decision'[2] or because 'they find themselves in an unfamiliar or novel situation' or they 'find the decision too difficult to make.[14] These young people do not lack capacity within the meaning of the MCA and are not covered by the provisions of the MCA.

If a clinician is considering treatment of a child and needs to obtain consent, they must first assess whether or not the child has capacity. The General Medical Council guidance[26] regarding individuals from birth to 18 years of age states that 'at 16 a young person can be presumed to have the capacity to consent' and 'a young person under 16 may have the capacity to consent, depending on their maturity and ability to understand what is involved' (para. 25).

If it is decided that a child does not have capacity, then consent must be sought from someone with parental responsibility.

16- and 17-year-olds who lack capacity

Parental responsibility is the right of a parent (or legal guardian) to consent to treatment if the child doesn't have capacity and the treatment is in their best interests.

A person with parental responsibility is outlined in the Children Act 1989 as:

▶ the mother
▶ the father, if he is married to the mother at the time of birth; or (from December 2003) if not married to the mother, the birth was jointly registered with the mother and his name is on the birth certificate; or if he has a parental responsibility agreement with the mother or a parental responsibility order made by the court
▶ a legally appointed guardian
▶ a person to whom the court has made a residence order concerning the child
▶ a designated local authority in a care order for the child (except if the child is 'accommodated' or in 'voluntary care' – section 20 of the Act)
▶ a local authority or authorised person who holds an emergency protection order in respect of the child.

To further complicate matters, if a 16- or 17-year-old doesn't have capacity to consent to treatment, a person with parental responsibility can make a decision only if it falls within the scope of parental responsibility.

This 'zone' has derived from the European Court of Human Rights case law and is difficult to define. The MHA Code of Practice[14] provides some guidelines, and the Department of Health and National Institute for Mental Health in England[25] recommend that in such cases the following are considered:

- ▶ Would the decision usually fall within parental decisions?
- ▶ Are there any indications that the parent may not be acting in the best interests of the child?
- ▶ Does the parent have the capacity to make the particular decision?

General Medical Council guidance[27] relating to children under 18 years of age advises that they should be involved as much as possible in decision-making even if they are not able to make decisions on their own. It stresses that competence is situation-dependent: 'it is important that you assess maturity and understanding on an individual basis and with regard to the complexity and importance of the decision to be made'.

It also advises that where children lack capacity to consent, parents can consent for them, but if the parents cannot agree and the dispute cannot be resolved, legal advice should be sought.

16- and 17-year-olds who withhold consent

An individual with parental responsibility does not have authority to consent on behalf of a capacitous 16- or 17-year-old who is refusing to do so. Possible options for gaining consent in such circumstances include common law, the MHA and the Court of Protection.

Even though 16-year-olds are presumed to have capacity (be competent) in law to give their own consent to treatment, it is good practice to encourage young people to include their families in decisions unless this is not in their best interests.[23]

It is important that doctors respect a competent child's request to maintain confidentiality unless significant harm may result.

General Medical Council guidance on refusal states that respect for young people's views about their treatment is important and points out that 'Parents cannot override the competent consent of a young person to treatment that you [the doctor] consider is in their best interests', but 'the law on parents overriding young people's competent refusal is complex'.[26] The GMC suggests that legal advice be sought if a competent young person refuses treatment that is considered to be in their best interests. It stresses the potential harm that might be done if the refusal is overridden and notes this must be weighed against the benefits of treatment.

It is important to note that the Court of Protection can overrule the capacitous refusal of a minor, including 16- and 17-year-olds, and authorise medical treatment.[28]

Children under 16 years of age

The MCA is not applicable to young people under the age of 16 and so the legal provisions for their medical treatment are outside the scope of this book.

CHAPTER 2

The Mental Capacity Act and the authority to treat

Implementation of the Mental Capacity Act

The Mental Capacity Act has been viewed as a far-sighted piece of legislation with the key purpose of keeping the individual at the heart of decision-making. Although there are many examples of excellent practice, some of which were presented in the evidence that came before the House of Lords Select Committee on the Act,[29,30] the Committee's report expressed concern about the patchy implementation of the Act.[31] In many instances, owing in part to lack of awareness and understanding, it is not well embedded in health and social care practice. Consequently, the duties required of it are not always carried out. A full list of conclusions can be found in the report, but recommendations include the establishment of an Independent Oversight Body to propel implementation of the Act. We will return to other observations of the Committee in subsequent chapters.

Section 5

The MCA authorises the clinician (or another individual) to act (or treat, in the case of medical treatment) so long as:

- the principles of the MCA have been observed
- 'reasonable steps' have been made to ascertain decision-making capacity and the assessment has led to a 'reasonable belief' that the person lacks capacity in relation to the matter in question
- the action taken is in the best interests of the person.

Because the MCA provides the legal authority to carry out acts in connection with the care and treatment of people who lack capacity to consent, it also gives legal protection from liability for carrying out those acts.

We discuss the definitions and determination of capacity and best interests in Chapters 3 and 4. Autonomy is preserved through the observance of best interests and recognition of the primacy of an advance refusal of medical treatment.

If the decision maker is negligent in their decision-making or treatment, they may be liable just as they would be if the person had capacity.

Acts covered by section 5

The MCA Code of Practice[2] lists the kinds of activity that might be covered by section 5.

Personal care

- ▶ Helping with washing, dressing or personal hygiene
- ▶ Helping with eating and drinking
- ▶ Helping with communication
- ▶ Helping with mobility (moving around)
- ▶ Helping someone take part in education, social or leisure activities
- ▶ Going into a person's home to drop off shopping or see if they are all right
- ▶ Doing the shopping or buying necessary goods with the person's money
- ▶ Arranging household services (e.g. repairs or maintenance for gas and electricity supplies)
- ▶ Providing services that help around the home (such as home care or meals on wheels)
- ▶ Undertaking actions related to community care services (e.g. day care, residential accommodation or nursing care)
- ▶ Helping someone to move home (including moving property and clearing the former home).

Healthcare and treatment

- ▶ Carrying out diagnostic examinations and tests (to identify an illness, condition or other problem)
- ▶ Providing professional medical, dental and similar treatment
- ▶ Giving medication
- ▶ Taking someone to hospital for assessment or treatment
- ▶ Providing nursing care (whether in hospital or in the community)
- ▶ Carrying out any other necessary medical procedures (such as taking a blood sample) or therapies (such as physiotherapy or chiropody)
- ▶ Providing care in an emergency.

The consultation and documentation required in relation to such activities in connection with treatment and care will relate to the consequences of the decision. Decisions of greater importance require a more detailed approach to the process and recording of decision-making and the assessments of capacity and best interests. For example, for an adult with a severe learning disability, choosing whether or not to wear a coat when going outside is generally (although not always) much less important than deciding about contact with a family member who may have been abusive in the past.

Notes

▶ Some decisions may be authorised under section 5, but extra care and consideration are required. Decisions that may have enduring consequences, such as a change of accommodation or major healthcare and treatment decisions, including 'do not attempt cardiopulmonary resuscitation' (DNACPR) decisions, may fall into this category.

▶ Payments: section 8 allows carers to be reimbursed for expenses incurred by acts in connection with the person's care or treatment. It does not allow the decision maker to help themselves to the person's property or other assets. Formal legal authority (e.g. lasting power of attorney for property and affairs, Court of Protection order or Court Appointed Deputy) is required to manage property and affairs.

The MCA Code of Practice gives guidance on the type of consultation that should take place in relation to these decisions. Consideration should be given to:

▶ the past and present wishes, feelings, beliefs and values of the person who lacks capacity to make the treatment decision, including any advance statement they wrote setting out their wishes when they had capacity

▶ the views of anyone previously named by the person as someone to be consulted

▶ the views of anyone engaged in caring for the person

▶ the views of anyone interested in their welfare

▶ the views of any attorney or deputy appointed for the person.

These issues might be best tackled by assembling the interested parties in a consultation meeting. However, the responsibility rests with the individual making the decision or providing the treatment. These processes will be discussed in more depth in Chapter 4.

If there is no one to consult and a decision arises relating to serious medical treatment or a change of accommodation in which the person will stay in hospital longer than 28 days or in a care home for more than 8 weeks, an Independent Mental Capacity Advocate must be appointed. The role and functions of the Independent Mental Capacity Advocate and the definition of serious medical treatment are discussed in more depth in Chapter 6.

Decisions outside the scope of section 5

Some decisions are of sufficient gravity that the matter should be referred to the Court of Protection even if the person has:

▶ a donee of a lasting power of attorney for health and welfare, or

▶ a Court Appointed Deputy.

Such decisions include:

▶ the proposed withholding or withdrawal of artificial nutrition and hydration (ANH) from a patient in a persistent vegetative state (PVS)

- ▶ cases where it is proposed that a person who lacks capacity to consent should donate an organ or bone marrow to another person
- ▶ the proposed non-therapeutic sterilisation of a person who lacks capacity to consent (e.g. for contraceptive purposes)
- ▶ cases where there is a dispute about whether a particular treatment will be in a person's best interests.

Cases may also be referred to the Court of Protection when there is conflict between the parties in relation to the assessment of decision-making capacity or a dispute about what is in the person's best interests. Guidance on referrals to the Court are given in the MCA Code of Practice[2] and the role of the Court is discussed in Chapter 8.

Limitations on acts permitted by section 5

The following can't be done under the 'general authority' of section 5 of the MCA:

- ▶ anything that conflicts with a decision made by someone with a valid and applicable power of attorney or a Court Appointed Deputy (assuming that the attorney or deputy is acting within their authority and their decision is in accordance with the MCA, i.e. in the person's best interests, etc.)
- ▶ depriving a person of their liberty (see Chapter 7 for the difference between restricting a person's liberty and depriving them of their liberty: the former is authorised, if necessary and proportionate, by section 5; the latter is not)
- ▶ restraining a person: this is defined as using force, or threatening to use force, to make someone do something that they are resisting, but:
    - ▶ restraint is permitted if:
        - ▷ the purpose of restraint is to prevent harm (to the person), and
        - ▷ the restraint used is proportionate to the likelihood and seriousness of the harm (to the person), and
        - ▷ the restraint does not amount to a deprivation of liberty
- ▶ restricting a person's freedom of movement, whether they are resisting or not.

The MCA Code of Practice[2] provides guidance on using restraint to prevent harm. For example, restraint may be used to:

- ▶ prevent immediate danger – a person with learning disabilities or autism might run into a busy road without warning if they do not understand the dangers of cars
- ▶ prevent potential harm – a person with dementia may wander away from home and get lost if they cannot remember where they live
- ▶ prevent harm to welfare – a person with bipolar disorder ('manic depression') might spend excessively during a manic phase, causing them to fall into debt

- ▶ prevent harm to the vulnerable – a person might be at risk of harm if they behave in a way that encourages others to assault or exploit them (e.g. by behaving in a dangerously provocative way).

These examples are helpful because they show a broad interpretation of harm beyond immediate physical danger or threat to health and demonstrate that the responsible actions of one who takes reasonable and proportionate measures to prevent these eventualities will be protected from liability. The following case[23] is illustrative of the issues.

ZH, a 16-year-old with severe autism and epilepsy, was with his carers on an introductory visit to a swimming pool. He became preoccupied with the water and would not leave the edge of the pool. His carers knew that he would be likely to react adversely to an unsolicited approach and advised the manager of the pool that they would take their other charges back to school and return with assistance to deal with the young man.

The pool manager called the police who, without consultation with the carers, approached ZH. One of the officers placed a hand on his back. ZH moved closer to the pool, a police officer grabbed his jacket but was unable to prevent him entering the pool. The water only came to the young man's chest and the lifeguards attempted to persuade him to come to the shallow end of the pool. Eventually the police used five officers to remove ZH and place him, handcuffed and with restraints on his legs, in the cage in the back of the police van.

This restraint was held to be unlawful because the officers did not consult the carers. They had not, therefore, fully understood the potentially serious consequences of using force and restraint on ZH. The court said that the police officers had failed to show that they reasonably believed it to have been in the young man's best interests to remove him from the pool in the manner they had done. This case also illustrates that deprivation of liberty may arise in a very short space of time if the restraint is complete (see Chapter 7).

Notes

- ▶ It is lawful to deprive a person of their liberty in order to give life-sustaining treatment or administer measures to prevent a serious deterioration in their condition while the authority of the Court of Protection is being sought.

- ▶ Because everything done with the authority of the MCA must be in the person's best interests, if the purpose of the restraint is solely to prevent harm to others, e.g. use of medication to reduce aggression rather than to prevent distressing restlessness (or self-harm), then it cannot be authorised under the MCA.

- ▶ Restraint might include physical restraint by carers, measures to restrict movement, or medical treatment to reduce agitation. In using restraint, health and social care staff must give consideration to its purpose to determine that it is proportionate. Returning to the principles of the MCA, the restraint must be:

- in the best interests of the person

- the least restrictive option available to achieve the reduction in harm

- a proportionate response, e.g. locking a person in their room to prevent them wandering out of a care home might not be regarded as a proportionate response; measures that are carried out for the convenience of the staff or the institution are unlikely to be regarded as proportionate.

▸ Clinicians, and other carers, are protected from liability for their acts in the sense that it is as if they have the person's consent, as long as they have taken 'reasonable steps' to establish that the person lacks capacity and the acts are in the person's best interests. So if, for example, they are negligent or use excessive force, they will not be protected from liability.

Common questions

▸ **Can the MCA be used to admit a patient to hospital?**

If the patient lacks capacity to make that decision and the purpose of admission is to investigate and/or treat, and provided that there is no conflicting decision-making arrangement (advance refusal of the relevant medical treatment or refusal by a health and welfare attorney or Court Appointed Deputy) and the patient is compliant, then the MCA can be used to authorise admission.

▸ **What if the patient objects?**

In the case of a patient with a physical illness (which is not the cause or consequence of a mental illness), restraint may be authorised to secure admission as long as it is a proportionate response to the likelihood and seriousness of harm that the patient might face if not admitted. If the patient requires admission for the assessment or treatment of mental disorder, then the Mental Health Act must be used.

▸ **Can the MCA be used to authorise the restraint and/or sedation of a delirious patient?**

If the patient lacks capacity to make the relevant decisions and the purpose of admission is to identify and treat the cause of delirium, then, given the serious, possibly life-threatening, nature of delirium, investigation and treatment could reasonably be believed to be in the patient's best interests. Consequently, measures that are a proportionate response to securing such treatment are likely to be authorised (unless there is a relevant and applicable advance refusal or refusal by a health and welfare attorney or Court Appointed Deputy).

Note that there are specific requirements if the advance refusal or refusal by the attorney involves the withholding or withdrawing of life-sustaining treatment (section 25 MCA; also see Chapter 5). A Court Appointed Deputy cannot authorise the withholding or withdrawing of life-sustaining treatment. However, if the person is to be deprived of their liberty or if their capacity is fluctuating and, when capacitous, they refuse the intervention, or where restraint or sedation is being used at least in part to prevent harm to others, then the Mental Health Act would need to be used (if the person meets the necessary criteria for admission under that Act).

The interface between the MCA and the MHA – which Act to use

It isn't always easy to decide which Act to use: the MCA or the MHA. It is commonly said that the MHA 'trumps' the MCA. It is true that when a patient is subject to the MHA, either as a detained patient or on a Community Treatment Order, then treatment for their mental disorder is authorised by, and subject to the provisions of, the MHA. However, the criteria for detaining a patient under the MHA include that it is necessary to use the MHA (for the patient's health or safety or for the protection of other persons), i.e. if the treatment can be given with the authority of the MCA then the MHA isn't necessary and can't be used. So a number of factors need to be considered.

If the patient is not already subject to the MHA

▶ Can the patient be given the required treatment under the MCA?
   (a) Is the patient 16 years old or over? Yes
   (b) Does the patient lack capacity to make the necessary treatment decision? Yes
   (c) Is the treatment in the patient's best interests? Yes
   (d) Is the patient objecting or resisting? No
   (e) Is there a valid and applicable advance refusal for this patient? No
   (f) Does the patient have a health and welfare attorney who refuses to consent? No
   (g) Does the patient need to be deprived of their liberty? No

If the answers are as above, then the MCA gives the required authority, regardless of whether the treatment is for a physical or mental disorder, in hospital, in a care home or in the community.

▶ What if the patient has capacity and is refusing the treatment or lacks capacity but the answer to (e) or (f) above is yes?
   ▶ Is the treatment for a mental disorder? Yes – Use the MHA.
   ▶ Is the treatment for a physical disorder that is neither a cause nor symptom or manifestation of the mental disorder? Yes – The

treatment cannot be given if the patient is 18 or over; if the patient is under 18, the Court of Protection could authorise the treatment even in the face of capacitous or 'Gillick competent' refusal (capacity in relation to decision-making applies only to people aged 16 and over; the equivalent terminology for those under 16 is 'Gillick competence', where a child has achieved sufficient understanding and intelligence to understand fully what is proposed).[27]

This begs the question as to what is meant by treatment for mental disorder. First, it's important to remember that the definition of mental disorder in the MHA is a disorder or disability of mind. The cause of the disorder or disability is not relevant. So, for example, in a patient with psychiatric symptoms due to hypothyroidism, treatment of the thyroid disease would qualify as treatment for mental disorder. Second, the MHA states that 'Any reference in this Act to medical treatment, in relation to mental disorder, shall be construed as a reference to medical treatment the purpose of which is to alleviate, or prevent a worsening of, the disorder or one or more of its symptoms or manifestations', i.e if the physical disorder is a symptom or manifestation of mental disorder, then it can be treated with the authority of the MHA. In one case[32] the court authorised the force-feeding of a patient who was starving herself as a consequence of borderline personality disorder. The MHA Code of Practice states that 'This includes treatment of physical health problems only to the extent that such treatment is part of, or ancillary to, treatment for mental disorder (eg treating wounds self-inflicted as a result of mental disorder)'.[14] In another,[33] the judge said,

'It cannot be disputed that the act of self harming, the slashing open of the brachial artery, is a symptom or manifestation of the underlying personality disorder. Therefore to treat the wound in any way is to treat the manifestation or symptom of the underlying disorder. So, indisputably, to suture the wound would be squarely within section 63. As would be the administration of a course of antibiotics to prevent infection. A consequence of bleeding from the wound is that haemoglobin levels are lowered. While it is strictly true [...] that "low haemoglobin is not wholly a manifestation or symptom of personality disorder", it is my view that to treat the low haemoglobin by a blood transfusion is just as much a treatment of a symptom or manifestation of the disorder as is to stitch up the wound or to administer antibiotics.'

All this suggests, for example, that a patient could be treated, under the MHA, for the consequences of taking an overdose if the overdose had been taken as a result of the patient's mental disorder.

▶ What if the patient lacks capacity but is objecting or resisting?

   ▷ Is the treatment for a mental disorder? Yes – Use the MHA.

   ▷ Is the treatment for a physical disorder that is neither a cause nor symptom or manifestation of the mental disorder? Yes – Use the MHA.

If the patient is already subject to the MHA

- Is the treatment for a mental disorder? Yes – Use the MHA.
- Is the treatment for a physical disorder that is neither a cause nor symptom or manifestation of the mental disorder? Yes – Use the MCA.

Entry, conveyance and transfer using the MCA/MHA

The two Acts give different powers in differing circumstances.

- If the person has capacity to make the decision and consents, then that is the authority.
- If permission to enter private premises is given and
  - the person lacks capacity in relation to their need to be taken to hospital
    - for the assessment or treatment of a physical disorder – use the MCA
    - for the assessment or treatment of a mental disorder and they are compliant – use the MCA
    - for the assessment or treatment of a mental disorder and they are not compliant – use the MHA
  - the person has capacity and refuses to be taken to hospital
    - for the assessment or treatment of a physical disorder – no action can be taken
    - for the assessment or treatment of a mental disorder – use the MHA (if the criteria for detention are met).
- If permission to enter private premises is refused, a warrant from a magistrate is required and the MHA can then be used (if the criteria are met).
- The DoLS Code of Practice[34] makes it clear that 'Transporting a person who lacks capacity from their home, or another location, to a hospital or care home will not usually amount to a deprivation of liberty (e.g. to take them to hospital by ambulance in an emergency). Even where there is an expectation that the person will be deprived of liberty within the care home or hospital, it is unlikely that the journey itself would constitute a deprivation of liberty so that an authorisation is needed before the journey commences'. In the unusual event that the journey itself amounts to a deprivation of liberty, it may require an order from the Court of Protection.
- If permission to enter private premises is refused, the police may be able to force entry under section 17 of the Police and Criminal Evidence Act 1984 (PACE) to save 'life or limb' or prevent 'serious damage to property'. The circumstances are likely to be where an immediate threat to life is anticipated.

▶ The police may also enter private premises where entry has been refused, with a warrant from a magistrate under section 135 of the MHA. Before granting a warrant the court would require the relevant medical evidence unless the person was already detained under the MHA and was 'absent without leave'.

▶ The MCA can authorise conveyance and admission to hospital, or transfer between hospitals, for treatment of a physical disorder if the person lacks capacity; the usual principles and limitations of the MCA apply.

Note

▶ There is no power available under the MCA for a police officer to convey a person from a private place to a hospital or other place of safety for the explicit purpose of treatment of mental disorder if the person objects. Only the MHA (sections 2, 3, 4 or 135) can give the necessary authority.[24]

▶ It is not lawful to detain a person under the MHA to one facility and then send them immediately on leave to another – for example, sending someone who is both physically and mentally unwell to a psychiatric facility as an interim measure to their immediate transfer to a general hospital.

▶ Standard DoLS authorisation empowers staff and provides sufficient authority to use proportionate restraint to bring a mentally incapacitated person back to the place to which they are detained, even if they resist, if it is considered in that person's best interests to return.[35]

CHAPTER 3

Assessment of capacity

Making decisions is a fundamental part of everyday life. Decision-making is affected by a complex combination of factors that vary between individuals and depend, for example, on beliefs and values that in turn are influenced by society, culture, education and pressure from family and peer groups. Understanding how an individual reaches a decision can be extremely difficult.

Despite this complexity, accurate assessment of decision-making capacity is the first aspect in the process of consent and is often crucial in the preservation of autonomy and self-determination. Studies have estimated that 29% of psychiatric in-patients[36] and 40% of acutely ill medical in-patients[37] lack capacity. This indicates that decision-making incapacity is both common and probably under-recognised. In extreme cases, for instance in impaired consciousness or more severe states of confusion, the degree of incapacity may be obvious; notwithstanding, practitioners must remain attentive to the principles of the MCA. In many cases where capacity is borderline, its assessment may require more careful and rigorous examination, including the application and interpretation of specific 'tests' or legal standards.

It is also important to be aware that decision-making capacity is not an all or nothing phenomenon. A person may be able to consent to a relatively straightforward medical or other intervention, but lack capacity to consent to something more complex. Furthermore, although the principle is to interfere as little as possible with autonomous decision-making, the degree of disability required to classify someone as lacking capacity varies in proportion to the gravity of the decision to be made. That is, the threshold for determining that a person lacks capacity depends, in part, on the consequences of the decision and resulting harm to that person.[15] This may make it very difficult for carers to decide whether a person has capacity to make an albeit unwise decision, or lacks capacity. For example, a person with a learning disability may be permitted to eat high-fat or high-sugar foods occasionally. But what if carers regularly allow this behaviour, causing excessive weight gain and serious comorbid physical illnesses? The risks become much graver.

Definition of and approaches to capacity assessment

Mental capacity is defined broadly in the MCA Code of Practice[2] as 'the ability to make a decision'.

The MCA codifies a 'functional' approach to the assessment of a person's capacity. This approach is combined with a diagnostic threshold to give rise to what is called the two-stage test of capacity:

▶ First, does the person have an impairment of the mind or brain, or is there some sort of disturbance affecting the way their mind or brain works?

▶ Second, does that impairment or disturbance mean that the person is unable to make the decision in question at the time it needs to be made?

Incapacity may be temporary or permanent and a person is regarded as unable to make a particular decision (section 3 of the MCA) if they are unable to:

▶ understand the information relevant to the decision

▶ retain that information in their mind

▶ use or weigh up that information as part of the decision-making process

▶ communicate their decision by whatever means they have available.

The more clinically conventional approach would be to establish that the diagnostic test applies before applying the functional test. That is, does the person have an impairment, and if they do, can they still make the decision? In the 1995 Law Commission report this was proposed as the correct way to ensure that the large numbers of people making unwise decisions were excluded from the decision-making process.[38] However, somewhat confusingly, the current state of the case law appears to reverse this sequence. Consequently, in assessing capacity the requirement is first to appraise the person's decision-making ability (can they understand, remember and weigh up the information to make and then communicate a decision?). If they are unable to make a decision, then, second, consider whether or not this is due to an impairment of, or disturbance in the functioning of, their mind or brain.[39] Whichever order these stages are taken, it is essential to be able to say that there is a clear connection between the two, i.e. that the inability to make the decision is due to the impairment or disturbance of the mind or brain.

When should capacity be assessed?

It is important to be aware that care and treatment are often ongoing. Therefore, judgement of decision-making capacity in these situations must be a continuous process rather than a single event.

More specific requirements for capacity assessment can come from a number of sources and settings. The situation may influence the approach taken to evaluation and the professional competencies needed.

31

A capacity assessment may be required because circumstances cast doubt on a person's capacity. It may be that a pre-existing diagnosis points to impairment or disturbance in the way their mind or brain works. There may be concerns that the decision being made by the person causes harm or puts them at risk in some way. Assessments also often arise when there is a difference of opinion regarding the most appropriate course of action, such as a patient's refusal of treatment or where there is conflict with other relevant parties, such as relatives.

Presumption of capacity

Although presumption of capacity is the first principle underpinning the MCA, the language clinicians use may suggest that this isn't their starting point when faced with a patient whose capacity they doubt. Two doctors gave evidence about the capacity of a 62-year-old woman with a 40-year history of paranoid schizophrenia (requiring several compulsory admissions to hospital), hypertension, poorly controlled type II diabetes and diabetic retinopathy, who developed a gangrenous right foot.[15] The patient initially consented to, but then refused, a necessary amputation. Both said she lacked capacity.

One doctor's evidence included the statement 'Currently she reckons that if she continues to dress her foot then healing might occur but was unable to clearly show that she had considered the option of possible worsening sepsis and death' and 'one needs to be certain of her capacity'. The other doctor said 'she is unable to fully understand, retain and weigh information'.

The judge said 'These formulations do not sit easily with the burden and standard of proof contained in the Act'. 'What is required here is a broad, general understanding of the kind that is expected from the population at large. [The patient] is not required to understand every last piece of information about her situation and her options: even her doctors would not make that claim. It must also be remembered that common strategies for dealing with unpalatable dilemmas – for example indecision, avoidance or vacillation – are not to be confused with incapacity. We should not ask more of people whose capacity is questioned than of those whose capacity is undoubted'.

Who should assess capacity?

Generally, if someone alleges incapacity, it is for them to prove it (see p. 2 for the MCA's definition of incapacity), applying a civil burden of proof, i.e. on the balance of probabilities (rather than the criminal test of beyond reasonable doubt). It should be noted that families and carers are not expected to be experts in assessing capacity.

To receive protection from liability for acts undertaken to provide care or treatment there must be a 'reasonable belief' on the part of the assessor that the person lacks capacity. The assessor must also have taken 'reasonable steps', given the circumstances at the time, to establish the presence or absence of relevant decision-making capacity. Expectations are higher for professionals qualified in a particular field, for example doctors, than they are for unqualified carers or relatives. Professionals should be prepared to conduct more detailed assessments and carefully document reasons for their assertions and the steps they have taken to maximise decision-making abilities.

For interventions such as a medical treatment, the assessment should be undertaken by someone with sufficient knowledge to explain clearly to the patient what they need to know, for example, about the risks and benefits of a particular treatment. In more complex cases, for example where there is significant mental disorder, where capacity is marginal, fluctuating or difficult to assess, or where the consequences of the decision are serious, it may be necessary to obtain the opinion of a specialist in mental health such as a psychiatrist or psychologist. Joint assessment with the professional responsible for the medical intervention may then provide the most informative evaluation of capacity.

Before the assessment takes place, it is important to ascertain whether there are any appropriately authorised substitute decision makers (see Chapter 5).

A clinician who is well acquainted with the person and their medical condition, such as a general practitioner, may be best placed to comment on capacity. Other members of a multidisciplinary team, such as occupational therapists, nurses and social workers, may also have the necessary skills. Sometimes, more detailed psychological or neuropsychological assessments are needed, particularly if there are specific areas of cognitive functioning that require closer examination or diagnostic possibilities to investigate.

Solicitors may be responsible for assessment of capacity in relation to their clients' legal transactions. Ultimately, there will be cases where the Court of Protection will be required to decide.

Details of functional abilities

There are no formal definitions of the different functional abilities relating to capacity. To help in their differentiation, the following sections give brief descriptions along with some suggested questions relating to medical treatment decisions.

Understanding

In the context of assessment of capacity, understanding is a complex process relying on the ability to perceive, assimilate and comprehend the nature of the information presented. It is a function of a number of cognitive processes, including intelligence, sensory abilities and the ability to sustain attention. Therefore, provision of relevant information in the most appropriate form is central to the assessment of understanding. The threshold will be the degree to which the individual appears to have grasped the information presented.

Suggested questions for assessing an individual's understanding of a medical intervention include:

▶ 'In your own words, what is your understanding of the condition that your doctor has diagnosed?'
▶ 'What treatments have been recommended?'
▶ 'What are the benefits of the treatments that have been proposed?'
▶ 'What are the risks of the proposed treatments?'

Note

It is important to use pictures, videos, examples, sign language (e.g. British Sign Language or Makaton) or other formats appropriate to the person's needs, if such aids will help understanding.

Weighing in the balance

Although the information that is 'weighed in the balance' is related to what information is 'understood', it is important to distinguish between the two abilities. In assessing what is weighed in the balance, professionals will need to determine whether the person being evaluated shows any acknowledgement of the condition with which they have been diagnosed or any appreciation of their situation. In addition, this element of the assessment focuses on problem-solving abilities – how the person prioritises competing options and considers the consequences of possible outcomes.

Whether or not someone believes the information that is presented to them may influence a decision, because of their flawed appreciation or insight into their condition or the treatment options. It may therefore be important to explore in detail the basis of beliefs and whether distortions arise, for instance, as a result of depression or other mental disorder, or whether judgement is disturbed by impairments in higher-order intellectual functions. For someone with a learning disability, belief of information may be based on as simple a situation as being told that it is untrue by a significant other (e.g. an older sibling, a peer or even Facebook).

A person's ethnicity, culture, gender, sexual orientation and religion may also influence values and preferences. In assessing capacity, assessors should be aware of the person's values and how these may vary from their own. However, if possible, the person being assessed should be able to account for the decision they have made or explain at some level the values being applied.

Suggested questions relevant to a medical intervention include:

▶ 'Do you think anything is wrong with your health?'
▶ 'What condition do you suffer from?'
▶ 'Do you believe that you need some kind of treatment?'
▶ 'What is the treatment likely to do for your condition?'
▶ 'What treatment has your doctor recommended and why?'
▶ 'What will happen to you if you don't receive treatment?'
▶ 'Why have you chosen treatment X rather than treatment Y?'

Expressing a choice

The mere stating of a preference does not mean a person has capacity, nor does failure to express one necessarily mean the person lacks capacity. Failure to express a choice may arise as a result of the severity of disabilities, such as coma or severe physical illness. Some may fail to express a choice because of speech or language deficits but may be able to indicate their preference in other ways. Some may be indecisive and vacillate over the available choices. Every effort should be made to assist communication and support decision-making, and only when these efforts have failed should a decision about incapacity be made. Be wary, for example, that people with autism may merely echo the last option that was said to them.

Suggested questions relevant to a treatment decision include:

▶ 'Have you decided whether to go along with your doctor's suggestions for treatment?'
▶ 'Can you tell me what your decision is?'

Retaining the information

The ability to retain information may be influenced by memory or attentional deficits. The term 'memory disorder' applies to various types of problem, but most commonly to the difficulties in recalling personally experienced past events or newly presented information that are typical in patients with some forms of dementia. Attentional disturbances may leave a person disoriented or easily distracted, and it can be seen in patients with delirium (sometimes called acute confusional state). Some people experience huge situational pressure when they perceive that they are being put on the spot by being asked questions. This can lead to such high levels of anxiety that attention is significantly impaired, and it is a particular problem for people with learning disabilities. Memory or attention deficits may mean that a person is able to make decisions quite adequately, but may not be able to recall them soon afterwards. This can be important, as consistency of decision-making when re-presented with the same information may be determinative of capacity. More detailed cognitive testing may inform how such deficits affect decision-making.

Practical aspects of capacity assessment

Preparing for the assessment

The amount of background information and preparation that is required will depend on the complexity and circumstances of the decision to be made.

First, be clear what decision the person is being asked to make. It may be a decision that arises in the course of your own day-to-day practice, such as one related to treatment or care. Or a request may come in the form of a referral and the nature of the decision may not be readily apparent. A request from a solicitor or pursuant to a court order should include some explanation of the legal test to be applied. In these situations, it is helpful to have additional information such as the reasons for a medical opinion or why the matter is contentious or disputed.

In an emergency, it may be possible to assemble only the most basic details. For more formal assessments of capacity there may be a number of valuable sources of information. General practitioner and medical records may have information about current and previous medical conditions, response to treatment, current medication, medical factors indicating risk of cognitive or functional impairment, as well as baseline cognitive testing (such as IQ assessments, statements of special educational needs and school reports) and neuroimaging information. You may be able to derive an impression of prognosis and the potential for recovery. This may be important if the decision can be delayed until the clinical condition, and thereby capacity, is improved. Although your assessment must be independent, there may be access to previous medical reports or assessments of capacity.

When appropriate, information from other professionals should be obtained. They might include nurses, social workers, care workers, care home managers and occupational, physio- or speech therapists. Functional assessments can provide objective evidence to compare with the patient's insight and their perspective of their abilities and care needs. In the context of capacity assessments, evaluation of activities of daily living (ADLs) such as grooming, toileting, eating, transferring and dressing, along with instrumental activities of daily living (IADLs) such as ability to manage finances, health and functioning in the home and community, may be important in deciding whether the person has capacity to decide on the care they receive or where they live.

Informants such as friends, relatives and carers may be able to provide indispensable information about a person, including their personal history; values and preferences; mental state and evidence of decline in functioning; current abilities and disabilities; and sources of support. But note that you should bear in mind the potential for conflicts of interest.

Plan the assessment as far in advance as practicable, making sure that you have to hand all the necessary tools and resources that you will need. A standardised assessment such as the Barthel Index[40] can provide a baseline level of functioning to evaluate activities of daily living. If formal cognitive testing is anticipated, consider which instruments will be required. For instance, will you use a screening tool such as the Montreal Cognitive Assessment (MoCA)[41] to provide objective evidence of cognitive impairment or will a more detailed examination be more appropriate using, for example, the Addenbrooke's Cognitive Examination (ACE-III)?[42] In some circumstances specialised neuropsychological assessments may be needed.

It may be necessary to confirm what time of day is either most convenient for the person or when they are at their best. Is there anyone else that ought to be present at the assessment, for example a trusted carer or friend, or an interpreter (ideally, not a family member) or speech and language therapist if there are communication needs? People with a low threshold for coping with questions because of high anxiety may need the questioning to be broken down into several short meetings or for the information to be collected by someone who knows them well and can ask the questions in a way that is perceived as much less threatening. All this takes time to coordinate but may be necessary.

To minimise the chance of inadvertently omitting important areas for discussion, it is useful to write down the topics and significant questions before the assessment. In some instances, once you are familiar with the available information, it may be helpful to consider where the person's capacity thresholds might lie for different decisions or how your questions will discriminate between their different functional abilities. This might help you explore areas of marginal capacity in more detail.

Do not be pressured into making a decision that will please the solicitor or the patient's family, or one faction of the patient's family, particularly one that is more persuasive or forthright. Be prepared to conduct, or recommend, repeated assessments if there is evidence that the person's capacity or clinical state is fluctuating or if the person is poorly tolerant of or easily fatigued by the assessment. It may also be important to delay assessment, or recommend a time frame for reassessment, if it is possible that capacity will recover with treatment. This will ensure that decisions are not made for a person when they lack capacity that would restrict or fetter them when capacity returns.

Conducting the assessment

The person concerned should be told the nature and purpose of evaluation and the decisions that need to be discussed. If the assessment is required for disclosure to a third party, this must be discussed and recorded.

In assessing capacity, it is essential to consider what can be done to optimise the person's functioning during the assessment. Depending on the requirements, this is another matter that may need to be planned in advance. Consider the following points:

▶ Good communication skills are required: make every effort to help the person to understand any decision that needs to be made.

- Minimise any sensory deficits, for example by ensuring that hearing aids are working or any appropriate audio/visual aids are available.
- Give the person easily digestible amounts of information and repeat the information with additional clarification if required.
- Take literacy and intelligence into account by presenting the information in a manner that maximises patient participation. For example, it may be helpful to have the information written down in short phrases or to use diagrams or pictures.
- Ask the person to repeat the information in their own words: this helps clarify both understanding and retention. Beware of direct echoing and lack of understanding, particularly in people with autism spectrum conditions.
- Be cautious in your use of language and how you frame questions, and avoid jargon.
- A person's difficulty in using or weighing information may be reduced by simplifying the choices presented, for example by dividing the choices up and presenting just two at a time.
- Non-verbal communication may also be important in establishing rapport and in assessing the role of anxiety in influencing decision-making.
- Be mindful of the role of cultural variables in decision-making. These include: ethnicity; religion; language; familiarity with and experience of institutions such as hospitals; and cultural differences in the provision of care by the family.
- Consider the influence of current medication on decision-making ability.
- Try to ensure that you will not be interrupted during the assessment.

Your questions will need to focus on the specifics of the person's different abilities. For example:

- Does the person understand the nature of the problem?
- Does the person know why the decision has to be made and understand its personal significance for them?
- What is their reasoning behind the decision and are they able to process information?
- Are they able to consider options and the consequence of taking a particular option?
- Can the person understand the likelihood of the outcomes and express a choice?

Take as much time as you need: it can be a lengthy process.

Mental state examination

Examination for abnormalities in mental state should proceed as in any other psychiatric assessment. It forms a crucial part of identifying whether there is any impairment in the functioning of mind or brain.

The presence of a psychiatric or emotional disturbance such as psychosis, mood disorder, cognitive impairment or other abnormality of mental state does not in itself indicate that capacity is lacking. However, when such disturbance is significant, as in severe depression, it may limit reasoning and judgement, and thereby impair capacity, especially with regard to more complex treatments or interventions.

Similarly, when the patient is delusional, for example as a result of depression or a paranoid state, it may be difficult for them to accept a specific diagnosis or the possibility that treatment will be beneficial.

It can be difficult to judge whether functional mental disorders in particular are sufficiently severe to invalidate a person's consent through lack of capacity. However, the task can be simplified if one clearly demarcates the different functional abilities. Take, for example, a man with severe depression who refuses ECT. He may be fully able to understand the treatment, retain the information and express a choice. However, exploration of his reasons for refusal may be telling. He may believe that he is not deserving of treatment because of some perceived previous misdemeanour or some other distortion caused by the severity of the clinical condition. As another example, consider a woman with anorexia nervosa. She may be knowledgeable about the condition and its treatment and be articulate in expressing choices. The critical questions in determining capacity may be whether she is able to accept that she has the disorder and to understand the potential adverse consequences of starvation on her body or the benefits of treatment.

Assessment of cognitive functioning in relation to capacity

Diminished capacity to consent is associated with impairments in memory, executive function and comprehension. Domains to be assessed in a cognitive assessment might therefore include: memory and ability to learn; attention and concentration; verbal comprehension and expression; and executive functioning.

A detailed discussion of cognitive testing is beyond the scope of this book, but it is useful to highlight a few areas for consideration. Table 3.1 gives examples of these cognitive domains, along with tests that might be employed for their examination. Many of the tests listed are not suitable for individuals who have learning disabilities, although they can sometimes be simplified. Alternatively, refer to their previous IQ assessments.

Memory is usefully distinguished into explicit and implicit memory. Explicit memory is available to conscious reflection; implicit is not. Explicit memory can be further divided into episodic memory (which relates to personally experienced events) and semantic memory (which relates to the storage of facts and concepts). Episodic memory may be divided into anterograde memory (the acquisition of new information) and retrograde memory (past events). Damage to different structures may preferentially affect different memory systems. Implicit (or procedural) memory refers to learned responses and motor skills. Note that use of the phrase 'short-term memory' is often confusing: it is applied to a number of different neuropsychological processes, so is a term best avoided.

Table 3.1 Cognitive tests that can be integrated into assessment of decision-making capacity

Cognitive function	Test
Orientation	Time (time of day, day, date, month, year, season) Place: Where are we? What sort of building is it? (e.g. are they able to recognise that they are in a hospital?)
Attention (only one test may be required)	Spelling the word 'world' backwards Serial sevens (counting down from 100 in sevens) Serial threes (counting down from 100 in threes) Digit-span task (repeating back a list of digits) Listing the months of the year in reverse order

Language	Fluency, articulation and grammatical errors may be assessed from general conversation during the course of the interview
	More specific tests may include:
	    naming objects
	    comprehension of single words and sentences
	    reading aloud
	    writing a sentence

Memory: anterograde	Recall of given name and address Recall of three objects after 5 minutes
Memory: retrograde	Recall of specific world or sporting events over past months, years or decades
Executive function	Letter and categorical verbal fluency (described in the text)

The executive functions are those higher cortical functions located primarily in the prefrontal regions that control a number of processes, including planning, problem-solving, reasoning, and initiation and monitoring of actions. Historical evidence and clinical observation are often superior to bedside testing for assessing executive functions. However, they may be usefully investigated using tests of verbal fluency. For the letter fluency test, the person is asked to produce as many words (excluding proper names) as they can in 60 seconds beginning with a particular letter of the alphabet, usually F, A and S. A score of 15 words per letter is normal. Category fluency is tested, for example, by asking the person to list as many animals as possible in 60 seconds. A score of 20 would be considered normal, 15 a low average and 10 definitive impairment.

Standardised assessments such as the ACE-III can be helpful in documenting the presence of cognitive impairment, but are no substitute for formal assessment of decision-making capacity.

In some circumstances, a broad assessment of cognition may be followed by a specific assessment of capacities. For example, financial capacity may involve an assessment of cognitive abilities, followed by more specific assessments of the individual's knowledge, skills and judgement relative to financial tasks.

Interpretation of findings and recording decisions

When the relevant information has been assessed and assessments have been conducted, a decision regarding the presence or absence of capacity will be required. There is no gold standard to compare against and the decision will be based on your clinical judgement. Many things must be weighed in the balance: the individual's diagnosis and prognosis; their cognitive, psychiatric and everyday functioning; their values and preferences; the risks inherent in one decision or another; the possibility of enhancing capacity by whatever means; and, of course, the legal standard for the capacity in question. In many cases, the judgement will be readily apparent. For example, if the individual has advanced dementia or severe learning disability with marked cognitive impairment and reduced capabilities in a number of domains, the lack of decision-making capacity may be obvious. The presence of capacity for the decisions in question may be similarly obvious in an individual with no or minimal impairments.

The most testing situation is when the individual occupies the 'middle ground': they have only moderate impairments in many domains, or have patchy but significant impairment in some areas but not others. A further tension arises by the seeming requirement to provide an unequivocal yes/ no answer for something that, in practice, often appears to be more of a continuous variable. The challenge is to consider all the information and weigh the evidence 'for or against'. It may help to specify the task more precisely, for example has the person the capacity to make a simple medical decision but not one of a complex or high-risk nature? Importantly, the decision must be based on a conscientious and objective assessment of the evidence. It should not reflect your disposition, values or preferences.

Your written record of a capacity assessment should note any diagnoses, both psychological and physical, that relate to the capacity opinion and explain their significance. Where possible, provide a clear yes or no judgement in relation to the decision, or decisions, that have to be made. If you find against there being capacity, you should record your reasons, including which abilities are preserved and which impaired. Also record measures used during the assessment to maximise the individual's ability to decide. In contested cases it may be helpful to document verbatim the questions you asked the person and the responses they made. Your record should end with any final recommendations and considerations, such as further interventions that would enhance the individual's decision-making capacity, the likelihood that capacity will return in the future, and the timescale for reassessment, if appropriate.

Conclusions and cautionary notes

Tensions arise between the requirement to have regard to statutory principles, the retaining of defensible documentation and the efficient provision of care and services. There are enormous resource implications if all patients are to have routine and detailed capacity assessments. This needs to be balanced against the possibility that professionals will be criticised if something goes wrong and capacity has not been appropriately considered and documented. Studies suggest that healthcare professionals document decision-making capacity infrequently even when there is a statutory requirement to do so, for example when the 3-month rule applies for those detained under a treatment section of the MHA.[43] Furthermore, although capacity can be reliably assessed using clinical interview and structured assessment tools,[44] striking differences have been observed in clinicians' decisions about capacity.[45]

Furthermore, the courts can be critical of professionals when it is perceived that assessments of capacity are in some way wanting. An informative case in this regard is that of KK.[46] This was a woman with dementia who, following an assessment that she lacked capacity to decide on her care and residence, was admitted to a nursing home. KK continued to express the strong desire to return home. During the DoLS process, various professionals again determined that she lacked the capacity to decide on her care and residence. However, the judge in the case concluded, on the basis of written and oral evidence presented by KK, that she did possess capacity. He was critical that she had not been provided with information relating to the appropriate and 'detailed options' for how she could be supported at home. Only in this way would it be possible to assess whether she had the capacity to choose between the available alternatives.

The post-legislative scrutiny of the MCA[31] has been critical of the behaviour of professionals in relation to capacity assessment. Medical professionals are criticised for making an assumption of incapacity in the case of physically disabled adults. Social care professionals are criticised for using the assumption of capacity to excuse inaction in difficult cases. Professionals are criticised for avoiding making assessments (to avoid legal scrutiny) and are reminded that the most suitable person to conduct the capacity assessment is the person that knows the individual best.

Finally, it is beholden on us to advise professional readers that assessments of capacity should be carefully considered. Be clear about what information is required for the decisions in question and, if incapacity is found, indicate which of the criteria in section 3 of the MCA (see p. 31 above) the person is unable to meet. Be prepared to give full reasons for your conclusions with reference to the relevant provisions of the MCA.

CHAPTER 4

Best interests

Clinicians must almost always act in their patients' best interests. The only exceptions are where the needs of others must take priority (e.g. because the patient presents a serious danger to someone else). What is in the patient's best interests, and how the clinician makes the decision, is usually a matter for discussion between doctor and patient. Sometimes only one course of action can be recommended. More commonly there are several options, with a balance between benefits and adverse effects. For the capacitous patient, the final decision is theirs unless they are subject to the Mental Health Act (see Chapter 9) or there is an overriding public interest. Having said that, it is important to remember that an adult patient who has decision-making capacity (and is not subject to the Mental Health Act) has an absolute right to refuse what you think is in their best interests. Also, doctors have a duty not to do anything that they think is not in their patient's best interests even if the patient wants it.

The MCA, while not defining best interests, sets out how clinicians should determine best interests for patients who lack the capacity to make decisions for themselves. Sometimes, as we discuss in Chapter 5, people plan for a time when they are not able to make decisions for themselves. However, this is unusual, and so the clinician's decisions have to be based on what they believe is in the patient's best interests.

The first question is who decides what is in the person's best interests? The MCA says the responsibility is that of the decision maker.

Who is the decision maker?

The 'decision maker' will vary depending on the person's circumstances and the decision that needs to be made. The decision maker is the individual who makes a decision for, or carries out an act on behalf of, a person who lacks capacity, and it is his or her responsibility to work out what would be in the best interests of that person. For day-to-day actions it will be the family member, informal or paid carer or nurse who is the decision maker. For medical treatment it will be the doctor or other professional who has responsibility. A social care professional will be the decision maker about, for example, a move into residential care or commissioning a package of care. If the decision is within the scope of the authority of a lasting power of attorney or a Court Appointed Deputy, then they will be the decision maker. Many decisions are made within the framework of the multidisciplinary team, but it is still likely that one person will have overall responsibility for the decision.

Family or informal carers are expected to have a 'reasonable belief' that the person lacks the capacity for the decisions – they aren't expected to conduct a formal capacity assessment. Among professionals, the capacity assessment will often be done by the individual who is proposing the course of action. There may be times when a professional, for example a surgeon proposing an operation, will ask advice from someone else, such as a psychiatrist, in relation to assessment of capacity. The assessment may even be undertaken jointly, but it is still the decision maker's responsibility (in this case the surgeon) to work out what would be in the best interests of the person.

There may be also competing views on the identity of the decision maker. Consider the example of an elderly woman with dementia who is no longer able to care for herself independently. Her husband wants to carry on caring for her as long as possible, perhaps to his own detriment. The children have decided that it is time for their mother to go into care. The general practitioner has offered an opinion that a care home is required and referred to the local community mental health team. The husband, the children and the general practitioner might all consider that they are decision makers (sometimes even before a clinical assessment or determination of capacity has been made). The actual decision maker in this case will likely be a social worker. They then have the unenviable task of orchestrating a process that allows all the relevant voices to be heard, tactfully reminding medical colleagues that they are there to provide an opinion, not to determine outcome, and remaining calm when some (or all) of the consultees are shouting 'Something must be done!'.

It can therefore be a surprise for families to find that, if they do not hold lasting power of attorney for health and welfare or are not Court Appointed Deputies, they are not allowed to make decisions for their relative. The House of Lords Select Committee heard that 53% of the public wrongly believed that they had the right to make end-of-life treatment decisions for their next of kin. The Committee also heard evidence that the medical paternalistic view of 'best interests' is alive and well, one witness describing best interests as 'probably the most abused and misunderstood phrase in health and social care'.[30]

What decisions are covered?

The MCA covers all decisions relating to the care or treatment of people who lack capacity to make the decisions for themselves. They range from whether or not the person should wear a coat when going outside to decisions about life-sustaining medical treatment. The decision may need to be made in an emergency or there may be plenty of time for consultation and discussion. Although the MCA does give lists of people to consult and actions to be taken before decisions are made, it is also very flexible. So, for example, an incapacitous person's previous values and wishes must be taken into account 'so far as is reasonably ascertainable', the decision maker must consult a number of others 'if it is practicable and appropriate', and so on. It is self-evident that for urgent life-saving actions such as securing the airway of an unconscious patient there is no time for consultation, check-lists or careful analysis of the decision. The needs of an incapacitous patient must not be undermined or neglected by the decision-making process. The decision maker is permitted, indeed required, to use their common sense!

Note

The Court of Protection determines best interests when the decision maker cannot reach a decision or conflict cannot be resolved.

How to determine best interests

The term 'best interests' arose in common law from medical evidence related to decision-making for people lacking capacity. Lord Brandon said:

> 'A doctor can lawfully operate on, or give other treatment to, adult patients who are incapable of consenting to his doing so, provided the operation or other treatment concerned is in the interests of such patients. The operation or other treatment will be in their best interests if, but only if, it is carried out in order to save their lives or ensure improvement or prevent deterioration in their physical or mental health'.[47]

It has to be, on balance, to the patient's benefit.

When advising patients, clinicians are trained to gather information from a range of sources and synthesise what is known about the patient's biological, psychological, cultural and family characteristics to diagnose and offer treatment. The clinician will advise the patient on the options available, perhaps offering a preferred course that they believe is in a patient's 'best interests'. However, professionals must not assume that, because they have applied this diagnostic or assessment process to a decision relating to a person lacking capacity, they are authorised to act. In health and social care, the difference between diagnosis and assessment on the one hand, and best interests assessment on the other, is that a person with capacity is able to decide whether or not to take advice from other sources (e.g. friends or the internet) and then to choose which option to take, or even to reject them all. In a best interests determination for a person who lacks capacity, the MCA requires (subject to reasonableness and so on, as discussed above) the decision maker to take those steps that a capacitous patient could make if they wished. These are:

▶ **To make no assumptions** Best interests must not be determined by assumptions about age, appearance or behaviour.

▶ **To take into account all relevant circumstances** It's important not to focus too much on specific professional considerations, such as risk (with which we all tend to be obsessed), which need to be balanced against the person's previous wishes, if known, and respect for personal autonomy. Institutional convenience must also be guarded against. The extent of consultation (see p. 48) and consideration that takes place in support of the decision will, of course, vary depending on the time available, the seriousness and complexity of the decision, and the availability of people to consult.

▶ **To think about timing** It is essential to consider whether or not the person may recover the capacity to make the required decision before it has to be made. Let's look at a couple of examples.

Imagine that a patient consents just to have his appendix removed. During the operation the surgeon finds a cancerous growth and thinks that the patient would want it removed. In this example, unless it is a true emergency, the patient can be woken from the anaesthetic and returned to a position where he has the capacity to make the decision for himself. This may seem to disadvantage him, but it is the law, which is why consent forms usually give a wider authority for the clinician.

A more difficult example is that of a woman with moderately severe dementia who is looked after by her husband. She becomes unwell with a urinary tract infection. She grows much more confused and disoriented, is found wandering in the street and is admitted to hospital. She requires intravenous antibiotics and rehydration, but she is acutely unwell and her physical condition is impairing her decision-making capacity. In such an emergency, it may not be practicable for the clinicians formally to consult relevant people before the decision to admit to hospital or to conduct investigations and treatment. It would not be in her best interests to delay these measures. The next day, when the patient's family arrive on the ward, she is showing signs of responding to treatment but remains more confused than usual. The family ask whether steps can be taken to place their mother in 24-hour care. The patient's capacity to make this decision has not been assessed. It cannot be assumed, at this point, that she will not recover capacity to make, or at least participate in, this decision, so this decision cannot be made at this stage.

Another type of difficulty is when, for example, a person with a learning disability appears to be able to make her own decisions when assessed in a clinical situation but shows repeatedly that she is unable to use that information at the time she needs to use it to safeguard herself.

▶ **To ensure participation** In many circumstances, the two-stage capacity test (p. 31) will itself provide a practical opportunity to involve the person in the decision-making process, as both stages involve giving information in a way that is most likely to be understood and processed by the person. By sensitively handling the information-giving process and involving those who know the person best, the decision maker may find that the person is able to make the decision or participate sufficiently to meet this part of the best interests test. The patient may be able to contribute to the decision-making process even if they lack capacity to make the actual decision.

▶ **To take into account the person's wishes, beliefs and values** The person's past or present wishes and feelings, beliefs and values may be ascertainable directly from the patient or through discussion with others. The patient may previously have expressed views about what they would want in a particular circumstance. The weight to be attached to those views will vary depending on all sorts of factors, such as how clearly they were expressed, how similar the current circumstances are to those previously discussed, how consistent the views were, how long ago they were expressed (views about treatment in 'old age' may be very different when one is 20 from when one is 60). In some circumstances, it will be possible to answer the question: 'What would they want in these circumstances?'. However, the best interests test is not a substituted judgement and often it will not be possible or appropriate to reduce issues to this question. Other questions, such as 'How would they approach this problem?' or 'How would they weigh up the options?', might help guide decision-making. Oral or written statements made relating to such a decision or evidence of how the person approached a similar decision in the past are particularly relevant.

As well as assisting the decision maker, understanding the way the patient would make a decision can help relatives and carers feel valued and relieve some of the burden of responsibility they may be feeling in relation to a difficult decision. Wishes, beliefs, feelings and values are not confined to the effect of the decision on the patient. Family members may fail to consider the person's feelings towards them, especially if they have assumed a significant caring role. It is important to consider whether the person would wish their loved ones to continue to care for them at the expense of the health of those individuals.

Where a person has a learning disability, it may not be possible to extrapolate a decision from previous experience of capable decision-making in health, family or financial matters. However, the knowledge of those close to the person should help the decision maker tailor both the process of making the decision and the outcome to fit the person's individual circumstances.

> **Note**
>
> Clinicians must pay particular attention to any statements that may represent an advance decision to refuse treatment – see Chapter 5. Even if the statement falls short of this standard, clinicians must record why they believe deviating from the recorded wishes of the patient is now in their best interests.

▶ **To consult others** Unless it's truly not possible because of the urgency of the decision, a number of people must be consulted:

- ▶ anyone named by the person as someone to be consulted
- ▶ anyone engaged in caring for or interested in the person's welfare
- ▶ any donee of a lasting power of attorney
- ▶ any deputy appointed by the Court of Protection.

The best interests checklist in section 4 of the MCA (discussed in Chapter 5 of the Code of Practice)[2] distinguishes between the person's past and present wishes, feelings, beliefs and values as reported by informants and the views of the informants themselves. Although the checklist places the person's views before those of the family or carers, the list is not hierarchical. When consulting family members or carers, the decision maker may find it easier to hear their views first, before asking about the wishes, feelings, beliefs and values of the person. Neither the MCA nor its Code of Practice advises practitioners how to use the information gleaned through consultation, only that it must be used in the person's best interests. This may seem rather vague and unhelpful, but in fact it allows the decision maker a degree of independence which favours flexibility and common-sense application of the Act.

The person may have identified someone they wish to be involved but not have made a lasting power of attorney. In many cases, the decision maker will need to seek out informants regarding this. The decision maker should generally ask the person who they would like to be involved in the decision. It is perfectly possible to be able to make a capacitous decision (although this decision doesn't have to be fully capacitous) about who you want as a consultee even though you lack capacity to make the required decision itself (we may remember and understand who is our spouse and that we trust their decision-making, even though we can't remember or understand the decision that needs to be made). Depending on the nature of the decision, it may be necessary to explain that this may involve the disclosure of confidential information. If the person is not capable of giving consent to disclosure, their identification of an informant as someone to be consulted should provide sufficient authority to share information needed to make the informant's contribution relevant, as this in itself is in the person's best interests.

What is to be done if the person seeks to exclude a relevant informant from the decision-making process? This is not unusual in situations where the person, though not capable of making the decision, is aware that another may hold information that might influence the outcome in a way they do not want. For example, a person with dementia who does not want to be moved to a care home may not want discussion with a family member who wants them to be in care. The decision maker must consider all relevant circumstances. If a plan is reliant on the cooperation of family members or carers, then it follows that their opinions are relevant. Indeed, the next group of consultees named is anyone engaged in caring for the person or interested in their welfare.

Substitute decision-making provisions exist in the form of lasting powers of attorney and deputies appointed by the Court of Protection. If either of these specific decision-making powers has been conferred, the donee of the lasting power of attorney or the Court Appointed Deputy will make the decision. If the decision is outside the scope of their decision-making they still must be consulted where it is practical and appropriate. For example, a family member who is the donee of a lasting power of attorney for property and affairs might expect to be consulted about decisions relating to health and welfare; an accountant would not. For further information on substitute decision-making arrangements see Chapter 5.

If there is no one for the decision maker to consult, other than paid carers, then an Independent Mental Capacity Advocate may be consulted. See Chapter 6 for more information on Independent Mental Capacity Advocates.

Best interests and restraint

When a care plan, medical procedure or act of care requires restraint, then the decision to restrain may become a significant factor in whether the care plan or treatment can be executed. If the person is to be restrained, the degree of restraint must be proportionate to the benefit of the act and the person must benefit from the care or treatment given under restraint. If restraint is proposed, its precise nature and the reason for it should be documented. The clinical team should consider what can be done to minimise restraint and to reduce its need in the future. If restraint goes beyond this, then a decision must be made as to whether or not the person is being deprived of their liberty (see Chapter 7). If the answer is yes, or in cases of doubt, an authorisation under the Deprivation of Liberty Safeguards must be sought.

The best interests meeting

The best interests meeting is becoming established practice in complex medical and social care decision-making. There are considerable advantages in bringing together all the parties to a decision. The meeting provides a formal structure for the decision-making process and a constructive way to approach and resolve conflicting views. For difficult decisions, it is reassuring for professionals to seek 'safety in numbers'. However, it is important that objective professional concerns do not overwhelm the subjective evidence from the person and those who have a concern for them.

The British Psychological Society guidance on the conduct of best interests meetings[48] includes the following steps.

▶ Identify a chair who is responsible for convening the meeting. This may be the decision maker, although there may be advantages to allowing the decision maker freedom to be an active participant in the meeting.

Before the meeting, the chair should:

▶ confirm that an assessment of capacity has been carried out and that the person does lack capacity to make the decision

▶ be sure of the decision that is to be made and the options available

▶ confirm that this is a decision where there is authority to act, i.e. a decision that is not excluded by the MCA (e.g. about marriage or sexual relations) or that can only be authorised by the Court of Protection (serious medical decisions)

▶ ensure that all the parties to the meeting have the appropriate information (the guidance does not suggest who should be invited and appears to assume that the person in question will not be present)

▶ ensure that someone among those present can give information on the nature of the intervention

▶ ensure that someone among those present can give information on the person's wishes, feelings, beliefs, values and any other relevant information. If there is no one, and it is a serious decision involving health or change of accommodation, then the chair must confirm whether an Independent Mental Capacity Advocate has been or will need to be instructed. The advocate's views, following discussion with the person, should be available to the meeting.

During the meeting:

▶ the chair should follow an agenda that begins with introductions and an explanation of the decision to be made and of how best interests decision-making works

▶ the chair might review that the requirements of the Code of Practice[2] best interests checklist are met, for example by confirming:

▷ that the decision maker has the authority to act on the advice of the meeting

- that the options available to the person are not being limited by their age, disability, behaviour, etc.
- that efforts have been made to enhance the person's capacity and to gain a view on whether they are likely to gain capacity in the future
- whether or not the decision involves life-sustaining treatment.

- those present should give the evidence in relation to their area of knowledge; in the case of family members and informal carers, this will be of the person's wishes, feelings, beliefs, values and any other relevant information; it may be helpful to record this information on a flip chart as it is given
- after all the information has been presented, the chair should conduct a discussion; this will include weighing up the advantages and disadvantages of the options under consideration in medical, social and psychological terms
- the chair should then:
  - summarise, perhaps using the information on the flip chart
  - ask each attendee for their opinion and the reasons for their opinion
  - point out that not acting is in itself a decision, and deciding not to act must also be in the person's best interests.

Further discussion may be required to clarify or resolve a position.

If a decision is reached, it authorises the decision maker to act. The decision maker is not obliged to act on the decision against their conscience, but must not frustrate the efforts of anyone who takes their place to enact it.

Recording best interests decisions

When making a record of the steps taken in forming a best interests decision it is essential to 'show your working out'. It is axiomatic that the detail and quality of this record should match the seriousness or permanence of the decision. There is also the consideration of time. A doctor dealing with a collapsed patient cannot be expected to record the same depth of consultation as a social worker recording a decision relating to accommodation.

As a clinician you may be asked to play either of two roles in relation to best interests. It is important that you are clear which role is required. You may be asked for your opinion on best interests by a decision maker (you may also have been asked for an opinion on capacity) or you may be the decision maker. In the first role, you should record your advice as if you were advising the person (patient) directly. Set out the choices, with the advantages and disadvantages, and indicate which treatment or care option you favour, giving your reasoning. As part of your assessment it is likely that you have made observations of the person's wishes and feelings in relation to the decision. These observations should form part of your record and communication to the decision maker.

Where you are the decision maker, you need to record that you have taken reasonable steps to establish that your care or treatment is in the person's best interests. The best interests checklist[2] will guide your actions in relation to assessments and consultations. This checklist should also be the template for your record. In routine clinical practice, a contemporaneous entry relating to each consultation will suffice. For more complex decisions where you have made extensive consultation, summarise the evidence from your consultations. It might help to draw up a table of the options under consideration and the evidence from the parties to the consultation. Make sure you record all the options or preferences expressed and don't exclude options that you do not favour. Recording the person's or consultee's own words in quotation may be the best way of illustrating wishes, feelings and preferences. Set out your reasoning for the decision reached. Tabulating the possible pros and cons of each option might assist your decision-making, as well as providing a clear record. You must also record your opinion on the timing of the decision and whether it is the minimum intervention necessary to achieve the desired effect. Where there is a best interests meeting, the minutes of the proceedings should provide evidence of the authority to act.

The most detailed record of deliberation on best interests will be required in reports for the Court of Protection. Guidance on preparation of reports on best interests for the Court of Protection is available.[49]

Conflict in best interests decision-making

The most difficult aspect of the decision-making role is resolving conflict between the parties to find a solution that is in the person's best interests and that all parties can accept. Delay in implementing a decision may be to the person's detriment and pursuing a resolution through the Court of Protection may be costly and time consuming. Most of the parties to a decision will have their own priorities and motivations and in some cases their interests will conflict with those of the person. It is worth examining these difficulties.

▶ **Institutional interests** Social workers act as agents of the local authority. The authority has responsibilities in relation to vulnerable people and it is not unusual for statutory measures to enforce risk-averse care plans. A notable example of a risk-averse council acting against the best interests of a care home resident is the attempt of Cardiff Council to use the Deprivation of Liberty Safeguards to prevent her from taking a regular cruise holiday with her companion.[50]

▶ **Professional interests** It is a matter of professional pride that doctors attempt to give advice that offers the greatest net benefit to their patients. It can be hard for doctors to recognise that a best interests decision can go against the best medical advice, especially when the skill of the doctor concerned is closely tied to the advice on offer, as in the case of surgery, for example.

▶ **Family members** Many factors can adversely affect the ability of family members and those close to the person to consult effectively with the decision maker. In medical decisions, they may struggle because they are coming to terms with their feelings in the face of their loved one's diagnosis. In decisions on care home placement, they are most often concerned that their loved one suffers no unnecessary harm and find it difficult to accept that a best interests decision may make independence a higher priority than safety or dignity. Family members with care responsibilities may sacrifice their own mental and physical health to keep a loved one in the family home even when that person might not have wanted their family to suffer for their sake. In circumstances such as these, children can be in conflict with the parent who has care responsibilities. Occasionally, motives within families are less altruistic. Children may be happy to see their parent's best interests overlooked if it means that the costs of care are avoided and their inheritance is preserved. Spouses or children who have suffered abuse from the person may find it difficult to resolve their conflicting emotions and focus on the person's present needs. In some cases, the closest family member may lack capacity to make the decision to go on caring for the person or to understand the concern relating to the decision in question.

Resolving conflict

The MCA is drafted in a sufficiently flexible manner for the decision maker to proceed without unanimous agreement. However, for many decisions the cooperation of those close to the person is essential for the execution of the decision. Where there is a conscientious disagreement or the decision is finely balanced it is unwise to ride roughshod over the views of family and others close to the person.

The MCA Code of Practice[2] offers advice about resolving conflict in best interests decision-making. A first step might be to rerun the best interests checklist[2] or circulate the best interests report to the people concerned before convening a best interests meeting. If this is unsuccessful, then the Code suggests:

▶ involving an advocate to act on behalf of the person who lacks capacity to make the decision

▶ getting a second opinion

▶ attempting some form of mediation

▶ pursuing a complaint through the organisation's formal procedures.

Ultimately, if all other attempts to resolve the dispute have failed, the Court of Protection (see Chapter 8) might need to decide what is in the person's best interests.

CHAPTER 5

Alternative authority – planning for the future

The MCA, in addition to guiding clinicians' practice when people lack the capacity to make decisions for themselves, authorises people who retain decision-making capacity to plan for a time when they lose capacity. There are two means by which they may do this:

▶ advance decisions to refuse treatment

▶ lasting powers of attorney.

These provisions allow capacitous individuals to make arrangements for a time when they may lack capacity. They are also known as anticipatory decisions. For the clinician, it is important to recognise when these powers exist and to understand how they apply. The substitute decision-making powers might be seen as mechanisms by which capable individuals can make or influence decisions that arise after they have lost the capacity to deal with them.

There is an additional substitute decision-making power in the MCA, which is provided by deputies appointed by the Court of Protection.

Advance decisions to refuse medical treatment

The terms 'advance decision', 'advance statement' and 'advance refusal' are often used synonymously. The important thing is to distinguish between advance requests for treatment and advance refusals of treatment. They all place a person who lacks capacity in the position they would have been in had they retained capacity (in relation to the specific treatment decision). A capacitous patient can request a specific medical intervention, but cannot demand it. Indeed, clinicians are duty bound to refuse to give any medical treatment that they do not believe to be in their patients' best interests. On the other hand, a capacitous person can refuse medical treatment and that refusal must be honoured. Hence, the authority of the advance refusal. The MCA is quite clear that 'the specified treatment is not to be carried out or continued' if an advance refusal has been made.

To make an advance decision to refuse treatment, the person must be aged 18 or over and have the capacity to make the decision. It comes into force only if they lose capacity in relation to that decision.

The advance decision does not need to be in writing (although it is obviously easier to be sure about the person's wishes if it is in writing), and if it is written it does not need to be signed or witnessed, with one important exception. That is if the decision relates to the withdrawing or withholding of life-sustaining treatment.

The MCA adopts a pragmatic definition of life-sustaining treatment. This is sensible because the same treatment in different circumstances may be life sustaining or not. Also, if the law were too prescriptive about what constitutes a life-sustaining treatment, it might not anticipate developments in technology. So the clinician is responsible for judging whether a treatment is life sustaining. Artificial nutrition and hydration are regarded as life-sustaining treatments. The MCA treats decisions to refuse life-sustaining treatment with special care and requires that:

▶ they be made in writing and signed
▶ they be witnessed and signed by the witness
▶ the person making the refusal verifies that it applies even though the refusal means that their life would be at risk.

Note

The witness is witnessing that the person has signed the statement. They are not assessing or witnessing that the person has capacity at the time.

If the person making the advance decision is unable to sign, the witness can witness them directing someone else to sign on their behalf (confirming this in writing).

It follows that when acting on such instructions, the clinician should be satisfied that the advance refusal is valid and applicable. They should record the discussion they have had with any relevant best interests consultees and copy the document for the records.

Making an advance refusal

The advance refusal can be made in layman's terms. Although the treatment to be refused must be specified, it does not need to be a single type of intervention: one can just refuse all treatment for condition x. No reasons need to be given.

The Code of Practice provides advice to those who may be considering advance refusal of treatment.[2] Refusals should:

▶ be made in writing
▶ give 'a clear statement of the decision, the treatment to be refused and the circumstances under which it applies'

- ▶ include demographic information and any distinguishing features that may identify the person should they be unable to identify themselves
- ▶ include the details of the person's general practitioner.

It is likely that patients will consult their doctor about making such a statement and clinicians should be prepared to assist in the preparation of a refusal if a patient asks for help (the clinician's terms and conditions of service may permit a fee to be charged for this). In circumstances where a patient seems unlikely to require an advance refusal it would be prudent to investigate the motive for the request. The patient may have hypochondriacal delusions or suicidal thoughts.

Clinicians treating patients with terminal or degenerative conditions such as cancer, dementia or motor neuron disease have a duty to give their patients appropriate information on the course and prognosis of their condition. These discussions, however difficult, do present an opportunity to talk about treatment decisions after the person has lost capacity. The clinician should take this opportunity to make their patient aware of advance refusals and the other substitute decision-making powers. Such discussions are likely to prove a worthwhile investment if the patient makes arrangements that help clinicians and loved ones when the time for difficult decisions arrives.

- ▶ A person can withdraw their advance refusal at any time while they retain capacity (in relation to the relevant decision); the withdrawal need not be in writing.
- ▶ Advance refusals relate only to medical treatment: there is no provision to refuse basic care, nor can a person refuse, for example, admission to a nursing home.
- ▶ To be put into force, an advance refusal must be both valid and applicable.

Validity of advance refusals

Validity is the legal standing of the advance refusal. If it relates to the withholding or withdrawing of life-sustaining treatment, it must be in writing, signed, the signature must be witnessed and the witness must sign it. The witness is witnessing the person signing their advance refusal. They are not witnessing its content or whether or not the person has capacity at the time.

An advance refusal will be invalid if the person:

- ▶ has withdrawn the decision at a time when they had capacity to do so, or
- ▶ has, under a lasting power of attorney created after the advance decision was made, conferred authority on the attorney (or, if more than one, any of them) to give or refuse consent to the treatment to which the advance decision relates, or
- ▶ has done anything else clearly inconsistent with the advance decision remaining their fixed decision, such as accepting, while still retaining capacity, the treatment listed in the advance refusal.

Applicability of advance refusals

Applicability refers to the specificity of the circumstances and the treatment. An advance refusal will not be applicable if:

▶ the person retains decision-making capacity, or

▶ treatment is not the treatment specified in the advance decision, or

▶ any circumstances specified in the advance decision are absent, or

▶ there are reasonable grounds for believing that circumstances exist that the person did not anticipate when they made the advance decision and that would have affected their decision had they anticipated them.

'Circumstances' can be taken in a narrow clinical meaning, i.e. 'does the refusal apply to this particular condition or diagnosis and the treatment proposed?'. However, 'circumstances' may also refer to life changes. For example, unless becoming a parent or being pregnant were specifically referred to in the refusal, then if this has occurred since the making of the refusal, the refusal might not apply.

Unless the patient told their clinician about an advance decision while they still had capacity, clinicians generally rely on informants to reveal their existence. The clinician will then need to judge whether what they have been told represents a valid and applicable refusal or a statement of wishes to be considered under 'best interests'. The test for the clinician applying the advance refusal to a decision is 'reasonable belief'. So a valid advance refusal will determine the outcome in circumstances where it applies. Note, 'in circumstances where it applies' – there may be good reasons for the clinician to consider that the refusal does not apply.

Clinicians are protected from liability if they stop or withhold treatment because they reasonably believe that an advance decision exists, and that it is valid and applicable. Equally, they are protected from liability when they treat a person because, having taken all practical and appropriate steps to find out whether the person has made an advance decision to refuse treatment, they do not know or are not satisfied that a valid and applicable advance decision exists.

Limitations of advance refusals

The main limitation of advance refusals is their specificity. They are useful for individuals who want to make clear their rejection of a particular treatment. They can help those with conditions for which specific treatment decisions are anticipated following loss of capacity. However, they cannot provide authority to consent to a particular treatment or to choose between treatments. The author of an advance refusal could not anticipate all the possible illnesses or complications that might befall them. To deal with these vicissitudes, the MCA provides a mechanism to confer decision-making powers on someone else – this is the lasting power of attorney.

Lasting powers of attorney

Anyone (the 'donor') is able to confer decision-making powers on a nominated individual (the 'donee'). This is an ordinary power of attorney. Such an arrangement could be made by a business person to give a family member or colleague the power to act on their behalf while they are away from the business. The problem with an ordinary power of attorney is that it ceases to have effect if the donor loses capacity. The Enduring Powers of Attorney Act 1985 allowed the powers conferred by a mandate to remain valid in the event of the donor losing capacity. The Act limited the scope of decision-making to property and affairs. You may still hear about enduring powers of attorney (EPAs), as they remain effective in relation to their donor's property and affairs. New ones can no longer be created, but an enduring power of attorney made before October 2007 can still be registered with the Office of the Public Guardian.

The MCA repealed the Enduring Powers of Attorney Act and introduced a lasting power of attorney (LPA). That is, an adult (the donor) can give the authority to make decisions on their behalf to another adult (the donee, or attorney). Both donor and donee must be aged 18 or over. The decisions may either relate to:

► health and welfare, or
► property and affairs, or
► both.

There may be one or more donees. They may be authorised to act individually or only together. The donor may also choose up to five 'people to be told'. These might be trusted friends, relatives or advisors. They must not be the proposed donees. These individuals are notified of the intent to register the lasting power of attorney and have 5 weeks from the notification to make an objection. This is a mechanism for the donor or their legal advisor to safeguard against a person making a lasting power of attorney under duress.

A lasting power of attorney must be registered with the Office of the Public Guardian before it can be used. There is a registration fee. The registered documents must include verification in the form of a certificate from an appropriate person that the donor understands the lasting power of attorney and has made it willingly and without pressure from others.

A property and affairs attorney can act concurrently with the donor, i.e. while the donor still has capacity. A health and welfare attorney can act only after the donor has lost capacity (in relation to the required decision).

For clinicians, the practical consequence of encountering an attorney for health and welfare is that the attorney has the same authority to consent, or decline, as the patient would have had, had they not lost capacity.

A lasting power for health and welfare must specify whether the donor wishes the attorney to have authority in relation to the withholding or withdrawing of life-sustaining treatment. Although this confers considerable power on the attorney, they cannot act outside the provisions of the MCA. It is important to understand that both the clinician and the attorney are bound by the principles of the Act. In particular, both must act in the best interests of the patient/donor. As a consequence, it might be helpful to think of the attorney, clinician and any other parties to the decision as a team rather than as antagonists. As well as being bound by the best interests principle, an attorney cannot deprive the donor of liberty, restrain them or make decisions about life-saving treatment in conflict with a valid advance refusal. These limits indicate the primacy of personal autonomy and the reluctance of legislators to hand over unrestricted powers to substitute decision makers.

The ability to make separate lasting powers of attorney for property/affairs and health/welfare allows the donor to nominate those that they believe possess the attitudes, knowledge and skills appropriate to the different decision-making domains. So one might choose one's accountant as an attorney for financial decision-making, and a friend or family member as an attorney for health and welfare decision-making.

Capacity to make a lasting power of attorney

Imagine a clinician consulted by a patient with dementia and her children. The patient has clearly lost the ability to manage her financial affairs, and her children cannot manage her affairs without the appropriate authority. This might appear to be a conundrum: how can she make a valid lasting power of attorney when she has lost the capacity to manage her affairs?

Before the advent of the MCA, the issue was considered by the High Courts. In two similar cases, donors had executed powers of attorney. In both cases there was evidence that they fully understood the nature and effect of the power, although neither was capable of managing their affairs. Objections were raised to the registration of the power, i.e. 'How can they make a power of attorney if they can't manage their property and affairs?'. The Court decided that a power of attorney was not made invalid by the donor's incapacity, due to mental disorder, to manage their affairs. The test was whether, at the time of execution, the donor understood the nature and effect of the power.[51] In other words, although a person may have lost the capacity to decide whether to consent to a particular medical intervention, they may still have the capacity to understand that their wish is to give their wife the authority to make the decision.

Bearing in mind that one must start from an assumption of capacity, for uncontentious lasting powers of attorney, the 'bar' for having capacity to confer authority to manage property and affairs should be quite low.

Making a lasting power of attorney is like making a will. It is not necessary to use a solicitor but many choose to do so. A lasting power of attorney must be made using the standard forms set out by the regulations. The forms can be downloaded from the website of the Office of the Public Guardian (www.justice.gov.uk/forms/opg/lasting-power-of-attorney).

Duties of the attorney

The attorney is obliged to act within the provisions of the MCA (particularly the section 1 principles and section 4 best interests provisions), but is also bound by a duty of trust and a duty of care to act competently. These duties, which are also set out in the Code of Practice, can be summarised as follows:[2]

- to apply certain standards of care and skill (duty of care) when making decisions – an attorney is expected to use the same care and skill that they would apply to a decision made for themselves; in the case of paid or professional advisors such as clinicians and solicitors, there is a higher expectation of skill and professional competence
- to carry out the donor's instructions
- not to take advantage of their position and not benefit themselves, but benefit the donor (fiduciary duty) – attorneys must be alert to any conflict of interest between the donor and themselves and act in the interest of the donor
- not to delegate decisions unless authorised to do so
- to act in good faith – the attorney should not take decisions that they know would go against the wishes of the donor unless they reasonably believe them to be in the donor's best interests
- to respect confidentiality
- to comply with the directions of the Court of Protection
- not to give up the role without telling the donor and the Court.

In relation to lasting powers of attorney for property and affairs, the attorney also has a duty to:

- keep accounts, which the Court of Protection may ask to see as evidence that the attorney has been acting appropriately
- keep the donor's money and property separate from their own.

The paragraphs in the Code of Practice represent the application of the best interests tests to the behaviour of attorneys. The attorney is expected to demonstrate high standards of ethical understanding and probity in decision-making. These are complex demands that even the most conscientious attorneys may find challenging.

Powers of attorney and the clinician

Once a clinician has established that a patient lacks capacity they must respect the decision-making authority of an attorney, if one has been appointed. Practical problems arise from this:

- How can the clinician know that a lasting power of attorney exists and what can they do in an emergency?
- How can they be sure that it is the appropriate power?
- What if they disagree with the attorney?

Clinicians are required to act quickly in emergencies, often with patients who are unable to consent. How can they possibly know whether a lasting power of attorney applies in these circumstances? The MCA allows clinicians to apply common sense in emergencies. They are authorised to act in their patients' best interests. This means paying attention to emergency medical treatment and stabilising the patient, not telephoning the Office of the Public Guardian to see whether an attorney is authorised to make the decision. In less urgent situations, the clinician must take practicable steps to consult individuals holding lasting powers of attorney (and other individuals who might inform a best interests decision) but not if delay would be to the detriment of the patient.

Lasting powers of attorney are meant to apply to the kinds of decision that have time for proper consultation to take place, such as elective surgery or care home placement. When there is time to consult over a decision and a power applies, the clinician must accept that the attorney makes the decision. If the decision relates to consent to or withholding of life-sustaining treatment, they must be sure that the attorney has been given the appropriate power, checking with the Office of the Public Guardian if necessary. Since both the clinician and the attorney must act in the patient's best interests, in most circumstances they will be pulling in the same direction.

Sometimes disputes arise out of a misunderstanding of the power. For example, the attorney may believe they can demand treatment that the clinician does not believe is appropriate. In this situation, the clinician will have to tactfully remind the attorney that even a capacitous patient does not have this authority over a clinician. Disputes about whether the decision is in the patient's best interests are a different matter. They should be dealt with in the manner set out in Chapter 4, including referral to the Court of Protection if appropriate.

An attorney for property and affairs might mistakenly or wilfully mislead a clinician into believing that they also have welfare decision-making powers. This is hardly surprising, as the provisions are complex. If the decision is not contentious, then the difference between a legitimate attorney and a party to the best interests process is of little importance. However, where there is disagreement about the decision, or the decision relates to life-sustaining treatment, the clinician must ask the attorney to produce evidence of their authority or call the Office of the Public Guardian to confirm that the authority exists. If it is found that the attorney is not authorised to make the decision concerned, this 'relegates' the attorney to a consultee in the best interests process and whoever is responsible for the decision has section 5 protection to act.

A lasting power of attorney may be cancelled by:

▶ revocation by a capable donor
▶ bankruptcy of the donor or attorney (for property and affairs)
▶ a decision of the Court of Protection.

In summary, finding that there is a lasting power of attorney for a personal welfare decision should be a welcome discovery, because this gives the clinician greater assurance that the patient's wishes are being respected and relieves the burden of the clinician's general (section 5) responsibility to decide and act.

Powers of attorney and accommodation

Note

If a person lacks capacity, a tenancy agreement may be signed on their behalf by someone who holds an enduring or lasting power of attorney. This also applies where a property and affairs Court Appointed Deputy has been appointed.

Providers of supported living schemes for people who lack capacity need to ensure that there is a valid, signed rental agreement.[52] Local authorities that place incapacitous adults in private accommodation need to ensure that the tenancy agreement is legally signed on their behalf or they may be liable for the rent (which would otherwise be covered by housing benefit).

The Office of the Public Guardian

The Office of the Public Guardian (OPG) is an agency of the Ministry of Justice. Its responsibilities, which include mental capacity policy and providing guidance to public, legal and health professionals, extend across England and Wales. Similar roles are performed in Scotland by the Office of the Public Guardian (Scotland) and in Northern Ireland by the Office of Care and Protection (Patients Section).

It is headed by the Public Guardian. It supports the Public Guardian under the MCA to protect people who lack capacity to make decisions for themselves by:

- ▶ keeping registers about:
    - ▸ enduring powers of attorney
    - ▸ lasting powers of attorney
    - ▸ deputies appointed by the Court of Protection
- ▶ supervising and regulating deputies appointed by the Court of Protection
- ▶ organising the work of Court of Protection Visitors (see p. 89)
- ▶ investigating complaints about attorneys or deputies acting under registered enduring or lasting powers of attorney
- ▶ working closely with other organisations if there are suspicions that an attorney or deputy might not be acting in the best interests of the person they represent, to ensure that allegations of abuse are investigated and acted upon.

Although it is largely concerned with financial supervision, the Office of the Public Guardian also has a welfare supervision role. The Public Guardian may ask for a report from a Court of Protection Visitor, refer the matter to the Court of Protection or involve the police, depending on the issue identified.

As mentioned above, lasting powers of attorney must be registered with the Office of the Public Guardian. Details of how to register, and the required forms, are available at www.justice.gov.uk/forms/opg/lasting-power-of-attorney.

The Court of Protection and Court Appointed Deputies

The Court of Protection and its deputies are discussed in detail in Chapter 8. It is worth noting here that the Court of Protection and, if appointed, a Court Deputy can authorise, or stop, clinical and other acts. However, a deputy can only make decisions within the authority granted by the Court. A deputy cannot:

▶ authorise restraint of the person outside of the authority of section 5 of the MCA (see pp. 23–25)

▶ make decisions if they believe that the person retains decision-making capacity

▶ make decisions that conflict with those made under a lasting power of attorney granted by the person before they lost capacity

▶ refuse the provision of, or authorise the discontinuation of, life-sustaining treatment.

If the deputy believes that a decision is outside the scope of the powers granted, they may reapply to the Court for clarification or authorisation.

The clinician and the Court Appointed Deputy

The duties of the deputy strongly resemble those of the holder of a lasting power of attorney. They must act in accordance with the principles of the MCA and follow guidance set out in the Code of Practice.[2] Patients who have a deputy are likely to be those with long-term conditions such as learning disability or dementia. The deputy, whether a family member or a professional, will be the pivot of the best interests process. The clinician's role is to advise what care and treatment is in the patient's best interests and, where appropriate, carry out the treatment and care.

Post-legislative scrutiny of substitute decision-making powers

The House of Lords Select Committee on the MCA heard evidence that substitute decision-making powers were poorly understood by health and welfare attorneys and Court Appointed Deputies and by professionals charged with taking account of their views.[29,30] The Committee recommended[31] that the Office of the Public Guardian address these poor levels of understanding and consider how information regarding substitute decision-making powers be shared between agencies.

CHAPTER 6

Independent Mental Capacity Advocates and regulation of research

The Independent Mental Capacity Advocate (IMCA) service helps support people who are incapacitous and have no friends or family to make important decisions for them. In relation to some decisions, such as those about serious medical treatment or moving accommodation (defined on p. 65 and p. 66 respectively), there is a legal requirement on NHS bodies and local authorities to appoint an Independent Mental Capacity Advocate to represent an individual unable to make their own decision if there is no one else to support them (statutory advocacy under the Mental Capacity Act).

These powers have been extended by regulations authorising the NHS or local authority to instruct Independent Mental Capacity Advocates in certain cases involving care reviews and adult protection procedures ('safeguarding adults procedures').

Put more formally, Independent Mental Capacity Advocates help safeguard the rights of people who are unable to make a decision about a long-term move or serious medical matter and have no one, except paid staff, willing or able to help them. The decision maker must take an advocate's opinion into account.

Local authorities commission Independent Mental Capacity Advocacy services, and responsible bodies (the NHS and local authorities) have a duty to make sure that there are sufficient advocates to be called on when needed. However, all advocates are trained and provided by independent organisations.

The advocate service[53] is provided for any person aged 16 years or older. Referral arrangements vary locally, but referrals can be made by telephone or email. At the time of the referral:

▶ the person referred must lack the capacity to make a particular decision
▶ the decision must be concerned with serious medical treatment, a change in accommodation, a care review or adult protection procedures, and
▶ there must be nobody who can appropriately support and represent the person (this does not apply to adult protection procedures).

In adult protection cases, a person with no one else to support them is entitled to an Independent Mental Capacity Advocate if the decision maker is satisfied that the person will benefit.

A recent review of the MCA included consideration of the role of Independent Mental Capacity Advocates. The report concluded that they needed to be appropriately trained and asked to be involved sooner and to a greater extent, and that people should be able to ask for an advocate themselves.[31]

An intervention constitutes **serious medical treatment** if:

▶ there is a fine balance between the benefits and burdens of treatment

▶ the choice of treatments is finely balanced

▶ what is proposed is likely to have serious consequences for the patient, for example if it:

    ▶ causes serious and prolonged pain or serious distress or side-effects

    ▶ results in potentially major consequences (e.g. the withdrawal of artificial nutrition and hydration or of other treatment which, if administered, would prolong life in a patient who is terminally ill)

    ▶ has a substantial impact on the patient's future life choices (e.g. interventions for ovarian/prostate cancer or sterilisation).

The MCA Code of Practice[2] gives some examples of potentially serious medical treatments:

▶ chemotherapy and surgery for certain types of cancer

▶ electroconvulsive therapy

▶ therapeutic sterilisation

▶ major surgery such as open-heart surgery or brain/neurosurgery (this excludes psychosurgery, which is covered by the provisions of section 37 of the MHA, irrespective of whether or not the patient is subject to the MHA, i.e. it requires the consent of a capacitous patient and an MHA second opinion)

▶ major amputations such as the loss of an arm or leg

▶ treatments that will result in permanent loss of hearing or sight

▶ withholding/withdrawing of artificial nutrition and hydration

▶ termination of pregnancy.

Note

There are some medical interventions that require Court of Protection decisions:

▶ withholding or withdrawing artificial nutrition or hydration from patients in a persistent vegetative state

▶ organ/bone marrow donation by the patient

▶ sterilisation for contraception.

In essence, the MCA says that serious medical treatment covers giving, not giving or stopping treatment when either the benefits of a proposed single treatment are debatable, or it is difficult to decide what the best treatment would be, or the decision is likely to have serious consequences for the person (this includes pain or distress, which are obviously extremely important considerations in someone with a significant learning disability, autism or dementia).

The following actions by an NHS body would constitute a **change of accommodation**:

▶ arranging for a patient to be accommodated:

   ▷ in a hospital for a period likely to exceed 28 days, or

   ▷ in a care home for a period likely to exceed 8 weeks

▶ moving a patient between such accommodation (for more than 8 weeks).

(The above points also apply to residential accommodation provided in accordance with the National Assistance Act 1948.)

An Independent Mental Capacity Advocate may be required for any decision where there are disputes as to the patient's best interests between, for example, family members.

Note

An Independent Mental Capacity Advocate is not required if a move or treatment is with the authority of the MHA.

The Deprivation of Liberty Safeguards (DoLS) extended the role of Independent Mental Capacity Advocates again, to support people who may be, or are being, deprived of their liberty. They must act if:

▶ an assessment is requested (by a hospital or care home) about a potential deprivation of liberty and there is no one else to represent the person: the advocate provides representation during the assessment process

▶ there is a deprivation of liberty by a hospital or care home and a request is made by the person (or their representative) for an advocate to provide support to ensure that the person has understood their rights

▶ there is a deprivation of liberty by a hospital or care home and there is (temporarily) no one to act as the person's representative.

An Independent Mental Capacity Advocate acting under the DoLS provisions has a legal duty of regard to both the MCA DoLS Code of Practice[3] and the MCA Code of Practice.[2]

An Independent Mental Capacity Advocate instructed under the DoLS provisions has the right to:

▶ receive certain information, which will depend on the circumstances of their instructions

▶ give information or make submissions to assessors, which assessors must take into account in carrying out their assessments

- receive copies of any assessments from the Supervisory Body
- receive a copy of any standard authorisation given by the Supervisory Body
- be notified by the Supervisory Body if it is unable to give a standard authorisation because one or more of the deprivation of liberty assessments did not meet the qualifying requirements
- receive a copy of any urgent authorisation from the Managing Authority (see p. 80)
- receive from the Managing Authority a copy of any notice declining to extend the duration of an urgent authorisation
- receive from the Supervisory Body a copy of any notice that an existing urgent authorisation has been terminated
- apply to the Court of Protection for permission to take a person's case to the Court in connection with a matter relating to the giving or refusal of a standard or urgent authorisation (in the same way as any other third party can).

In general terms, an advocate helps someone to express their views and feelings, make choices and be informed of their rights. Advocates are independent of other services/carers and work on a one-to-one basis. People using the Independent Mental Capacity Advocacy service may have communication difficulties preventing them from instructing an advocate or expressing a view about a proposed decision. In such circumstances, an advocate uses non-instructed advocacy. This is where an advocate goes to meetings on the person's behalf and considers any proposed decisions to make sure that all options have been considered. Where possible, the person's preferences and dislikes are taken into account, there are no individual/personal motives, and the person's civil, human and welfare rights are respected.

Independent Mental Capacity Advocates do not make decisions nor do they offer their own opinion. Advocates identify how the person prefers to communicate, meet them and attempt to ascertain their views, consult others, gather relevant information and attend meetings. They may raise issues as appropriate, and provide the decision maker with verbal and written reports. They may also audit the best interests decision-making process and challenge any decision. They help ensure that the wider view of any situation is considered and perhaps that clinicians reassess their treatment decisions in the light of often probing questions about best interests, backed up by access to records and researched information. Advocates remain involved until the decision is made, to ensure that vulnerable people do not get lost in the system – their dogged requests for updates reduces the risk of slippage or lost appointments. By providing an independent, informed viewpoint, Independent Mental Capacity Advocates can improve the quality of clinical decisions made in the patient's best interests.

If a person already has someone to speak for them, they may still be entitled to an Independent Mental Capacity Advocate, who would consult that individual.

There is no need to instruct an Independent Mental Capacity Advocate if a personal welfare attorney, a Court Appointed Deputy or someone else has already been nominated to be consulted on the specific issue.

The Department of Health's review of the Independent Mental Capacity Advocacy service in 2009–2010 notes that 'there are still wide disparities in the rate of IMCA instructions across different local authorities which cannot wholly be explained by population differences. It is likely that some people are not referred to an IMCA, particularly when serious medical treatment decisions are being made'.[54]

Research under the MCA

Before the MCA came into force, research involving people who lacked the capacity to consent was legally difficult. Anything done to a person had to be in their best interests. So, unless it could be argued that participants themselves would benefit – not that common a situation – the research may have been unlawful.

Sections 30–34 of the MCA give a clear framework for lawful research. The Act does not itself define research, but the Code of Practice refers to a Department of Health definition: 'Research can be defined as the attempt to derive generalisable new knowledge by addressing clearly defined questions with systematic and rigorous methods'.[55] Incapacitous participants might be recruited for research attempting to answer questions relating to the biology, epidemiology, treatment and care of conditions that may affect mental capacity, and research into emergency medicine, anaesthetics and surgical specialties, as well as mental health and social care.

The MCA gives a pragmatic definition of intrusive research as research that would be unlawful if it was carried out without person's consent. Intrusive research cannot be carried out without the approval of an 'appropriate body' (see below).

Regulation of research in the National Health Service

The Research Governance Framework for Health and Social Care[55] governs all research taking place within the NHS. It has made Research Ethics Committees (RECs) mandatory and places the duty to obtain informed consent at the heart of ethical research. The MCA provides the authority for researchers to act where consent cannot be obtained. The MCA and the Research Governance Framework together cover most of the research likely to be undertaken by NHS clinicians and social care researchers where the individuals involved lack capacity to consent to participation.

The appropriate body is the 'person, committee or other body specified in the related regulations[56] – in the NHS this is the particular Research Ethics Committee.

Requirements for research

To authorise research, the appropriate body must be satisfied that a number of requirements are met. The research:

▶ must be connected with an 'impairing condition' affecting the proposed participant or its treatment – an 'impairing condition' is a condition that is (or may be) attributable or causally related to an impairment or disturbance in function of the mind or brain; put simply, the research must be related to the person's disorder

▶ must not be possible on a person who could consent

▶ must:

  ▷ have potential benefit for the person and that benefit must outweigh any burden to them, or

  ▷ be intended to provide knowledge about the impairing condition, and the risk and burden to the person must be negligible and there must be minimal restriction of their freedom and privacy.

Measures must also be in place to ensure consultation and safeguards.

Taken together, these requirements mean that the appropriate body must possess, or have access to, expertise in the area of study in order to scrutinise a proposal properly.

Consultation

The consultation process for research is analogous to the best interests consultation for health and social care decisions, albeit with the identification of one consultee per participant. A researcher conducting an approved research project must establish a process of consultation for each participant in order for research to be authorised.

The consultation process

▶ The researcher must take reasonable steps to identify a suitable consultee or, in accordance with guidance issued by the appropriate authority, nominate a consultee.

▶ The consultee must not be a paid carer or have a connection with the project. They must be prepared to be consulted.

▶ The researcher must provide appropriate information to the consultee and, in the light of this, ask the consultee what the proposed person's views on participation might be if they had capacity. The researcher must also ask the consultee's advice about whether to enrol the proposed person.

▶ The person must not be entered into the study, or must be withdrawn, if the consultee informs the researcher that, in their opinion, the person's wishes and feelings would have led them to decline or withdraw. The researcher should continue treatment administered as part of the study if withdrawal would pose a significant risk to the person's health.

▶ The donee of a lasting power of attorney, or a Court Appointed Deputy, can be used as a consultee.

▶ If the research relates to emergencies, e.g. studies of treatments for serious injuries, there may not be time to appoint a consultee and canvas their views before enrolment in the research. In these circumstances enrolment can proceed:

▷ with the agreement of a medical practitioner who is not part of the trial, or, if that is not possible,

▷ if the researcher follows the procedure set out by the appropriate body.

▶ The researcher cannot rely on the provisions for urgent approval if they have a reasonable belief that the urgent conditions are no longer satisfied.

Safeguards

The researcher must:

▶ always place the best interests of the individual above the interests of science or society

▶ take into account the individual's previous/current wishes and feelings if known

▶ not do anything to which the individual objects; the exception to this is where what is being done is intended to protect the individual or prevent harm or discomfort

▶ respect any advance refusal of medical treatment or statement made in respect of any component of the intervention

▶ withdraw the individual if they appear to be objecting or if the requirements authorising the research are no longer met.

Clinical trials

Clinical trials are not considered to be 'research' under the provisions of the MCA (section 30(3)). Clinical trials are intended to:

▶ discover or verify the clinical, pharmacological or other pharmacodynamic effects of one or more medicinal products

▶ identify adverse reactions to one or more such products, or

▶ study absorption, distribution, metabolism and excretion of one or more such products with the object of ascertaining the safety or efficacy of those products.

Clinical trials are regulated by the Medicines for Human Use (Clinical Trials) Regulations 2004. The provisions (schedule 1, part 5) relating to consent for incapacitous individuals allow consent to be obtained via the person's 'legal representative'. This is a different mechanism from the MCA test of best interests. The 'legal representative' can be:

► the person's doctor
► the donee of a lasting power of attorney for health and welfare
► a suitably enabled deputy of the Court of Protection.

The regulations protect the interests of the incapacitous person by setting out strict principles, including:

► the primacy of the person's interests over those of science and society
► the right to receive relevant information
► the right of withdrawal
► that the presumed benefit must outweigh any risk or be of no risk at all, and
► that the trial is essential to validate data obtained from participants who can give informed consent.

Human Tissue Act 2004

The Human Tissue Act provides for consent by capacitous individuals for retention of their tissue for research. There is no authority under the Human Tissue Act for retention of tissue from incapacitous individuals (it pre-dates the MCA). However, if a trial that is properly approved under the research provisions of the MCA includes retention of tissue from an incapacitous individual, then the individual is presumed to have consented for the purposes of the Human Tissue Act.

Personal Genome Project UK

Although not strictly research, the Personal Genome Project UK is planning to recruit 100 000 British volunteers who are over 21 years of age and capable of giving consent to have their DNA sequenced and published online. The project aims to contribute to advances in medical science, including learning more about Alzheimer's disease and genetic syndromes – conditions that often affect people who may be unable to consent.

CHAPTER 7

Deprivation of Liberty Safeguards

Deprivation of liberty

The MCA, as described so far, makes it clear that it cannot authorise a person to be deprived of their liberty. In April 2008, the Deprivation of Liberty Safeguards (DoLS) were added to the MCA. The purpose was to resolve the incompatibility between English and Welsh law and European law established by the European Court of Human Rights case known as 'Bournewood' (more properly *HL v United Kingdom*).[57] The DoLS provide a procedure for authorising deprivation of liberty, as required by Article 5 of the European Convention on Human Rights, in particular situations:

▶ where an individual, 18 years of age or over, suffers from a mental disorder and lacks the capacity to consent to care or treatment, and

▶ the circumstances of their care within a care home or hospital amount to deprivation of liberty, and

▶ this deprivation of liberty is deemed necessary in their best interests.

Notes

▶ The MCA applies to people aged 16 and over, but the DoLS provisions apply only to those aged 18 and over. This is because the Children Act 1989 can be used to authorise deprivation of liberty for those under 18.

▶ DoLS cannot be used to deprive a person of their liberty in their own home. Only the Court of Protection can authorise this. This includes people in supported living arrangements where they have a tenancy agreement.

The DoLS provisions provide an additional legal framework that affords greater protection for mentally incapacitated people who require a high level of care, whether in hospital or elsewhere, but who fall outside the scope of the MHA. The DoLS scheme authorises detention in a range of situations and for a variety of purposes. However, the first consideration is what constitutes a deprivation of someone's liberty? The previous edition of this book discussed in some detail how case law had developed to inform the factors that clinicians and others must consider in order to recognise, and if possible prevent, deprivation of liberty. There was no statutory definition of the concept and, although there was guidance in the DoLS Code of Practice,[3] the emergent cases were unable to resolve the ambiguity. The detail-specific nature of the cases and differences in judicial interpretation meant that concepts were not readily generalisable and, without sufficient clarity, the so-called 'Bournewood gap' (see below) remained open. Thereby many compliant but mentally incapacitated individuals in a range of settings were not afforded any protective safeguards under the law. This degree of uncertainty about the meaning of deprivation of liberty was amply demonstrated by the failure of professional groups, including experts in the field, to agree on when it may be happening.[58] To put it bluntly, no one could be certain about the boundary between restriction and deprivation of liberty. The judgment in the Cheshire West case,[59] discussed below, was the Supreme Court's attempt to clarify this contentious area of law.

Bournewood and the guiding principles

A useful starting point is to examine briefly the circumstances of the case of Mr L and his care and treatment at Bournewood Hospital.[57]

► Mr L was 48 at the time of the events and had suffered from severe learning disabilities and autism from birth; he was unable to speak and his disabilities were such that he lacked capacity to consent to medical treatment.

► He was frequently agitated and had a history of self-harm.

► He had been cared for at Bournewood Hospital for 30 years and then discharged to paid carers (Mr and Mrs E), who felt able to manage his behaviour.

► One day, Mr L became disturbed at the day centre he attended. He was hitting himself on the head and banging his head against a wall. This incident resulted in his informal readmission to Bournewood Hospital to re-evaluate his treatment plan.

► He acquiesced to the treatment regime and made no attempts to leave the hospital (it was clear that he would have been detained under the MHA had he tried to do so).

► The doors of the ward were not locked.

► The treating psychiatrist judged that it was unwise for Mr and Mrs E to visit in case Mr L thought that he could go home with them following each visit. No discharge date was specified.

► Mr and Mrs E wanted to take him home, but they were told they could not do so.

The authority for Mr L's admission was justified under common law. The legality of this was considered in the English courts. There were two separate issues. First, was he deprived of his liberty? Second, if so, was it lawful to do this using common law? The High Court said that he wasn't deprived; the Court of Appeal said that he was and should have been detained under the MHA; the Law Lords said he wasn't deprived, but if he had been, the common law would have authorised the deprivation. Ultimately, the judgment of the European Court (in October 2004) was that Mr L had been deprived of his liberty within the meaning of Article 5 (the right to liberty and security) of the European Convention on Human Rights and that the deprivation had not been 'in accordance with a procedure prescribed by law' (violating Article 5(1)). Further, the procedures available to review the legality of his detention did not satisfy the requirements of Article 5(4). Whether the ward was 'locked' or 'lockable' was not considered determinative of deprivation of liberty, because everyone was clear that had Mr L tried to leave, he would have been prevented from doing so. Importantly, the Court concluded that healthcare professionals had exercised 'complete and effective control' over his care and movements. It was therefore apparent that his admission to hospital was achieved despite the expressed wishes of his carers, who were willing and able to provide an alternative to hospital care. In addition, the care regime to which he was subject in hospital was more restrictive than it need have been.

Following the Court of Appeal judgment, Mr L was detained under the MHA. He appealed against his detention to the Hospital Managers and was discharged – getting his freedom back. This perhaps demonstrates the importance of having 'a procedure prescribed by law' (which, to be compliant with the European Convention, must include a right of appeal).

Further developments from case law

There is now a wealth of case law from the Court of Protection in relation to DoLS. Some guidance which continues to be relevant comes from the case of DE.[60] The circumstances were that Mr DE was free to leave the care home in which he had been placed (against his incapacitous wishes and the wishes of his wife) in as much as he was allowed to go out on excursions provided by the care home. However, the judge said that the fundamental issue in considering whether deprivation of liberty was occurring was Mr DE's freedom to leave 'in the sense of removing himself permanently in order to live where and with whom he chooses, specifically removing himself to live at home with Mrs JE'.

In concluding that Mr DE was deprived of his liberty, the judge emphasised the three conditions that must be satisfied in order for a deprivation of liberty to occur:

1   the starting point will be the concrete situation of the case concerned (the 'objective element' of a person's confinement)
2   second is whether the person has not validly consented to the confinement in question (the 'subjective element')
3   third is whether the public authorities are directly or indirectly involved in the person's detention (that the deprivation is 'imputable to the

State'; this is because the European Convention on Human Rights applies only to States and their agents).

Imputability to the State

The ways in which the State may be responsible for a person's confinement may be summarised as follows. First, Article 5 may be engaged by the direct involvement of the public authorities in the person's deprivation of liberty if it takes place in a hospital or care home run by a public authority (or a private hospital/care home acting on behalf of the State). Second, there is an obligation on the State, through the local authority, to take positive steps to protect people from such interference by other private individuals.

For example, a doctor, when treating an NHS patient, or a private patient on behalf of the State, acts as a public authority and any deprivation of liberty would be imputable to the State. This is not the case when treating a paying private patient (unless using the authority of the MCA or MHA).

There is another important aspect of 'imputability to the State'. It has been suggested, for example, that a patient in a persistent vegetative state should be made subject to DoLS because they are being deprived of their liberty. We would suggest that the State is not responsible for depriving such a patient of their liberty. Indeed, the State would be delighted if a patient in a persistent vegetative state could get up and leave the hospital (at the time of writing there has not been a case to test this suggestion).

The Cheshire West case

Despite the wealth of case law from the Court of Protection in relation to DoLS it was a judgment handed down by the Supreme Court in March 2014 that provided a measure of clarity.[59] The Court considered the cases of three people with learning disabilities, heard together over a three-day hearing in October 2013. The cases concerned two sisters, P and Q (originally known as MIG and MEG), and a man, P. Taking the lead in what has become known as the Cheshire West judgment, Lady Hale clearly articulated what the Court had to decide: 'This case is about the criteria for judging whether the living arrangements made for a mentally incapacitated person amount to a deprivation of liberty. If they do, then the deprivation has to be authorised, either by a court or by the procedures known as the deprivation of liberty safeguards, set out in the Mental Capacity Act 2005'.[59] What is called the 'acid test' in deciding whether someone is deprived of their liberty is discussed on p. 78.

Background to the cases

'P and Q'
Born in 1991 and 1992, P and Q are sisters, both with learning disabilities, who lived with their mother, sister and half-sister, until they were removed in April 2007. The life of P and Q in the family home was described as

'dysfunctional and abusive'.[62] The severity of their impairments meant that both P and Q were unable to make relevant decisions for themselves, they both needed a high degree of supervision in their respective environments and they had no safety awareness. Details of their situations are summarised in Box 7.1. Their joint case had been previously considered in the Court of Protection and the Court of Appeal. Neither court found either of them to be deprived of their liberty.[61,62]

'P' (in Cheshire West)

P was 38 at the time of the Court of Protection hearing.[63] He was born with cerebral palsy and Down syndrome with significant physical and learning disabilities and he had a history of cerebrovascular accidents. He required around the clock care to meet his substantial personal needs. The details

---

Box 7.1 The situation of P and Q

About P

- P's learning disability is described as being on the border between moderate and severe
- She has problems with her sight and with her hearing
- P's communication is limited and she spends much of her time listening to music on her iPod
- In 2007, P was moved into a foster home
- She never attempted to leave the home by herself and showed no wish to do so
- She received no medication
- She attended a further education unit daily during term time
- She was taken on trips and holidays by her foster mother
- She had very limited social life

About Q

- Q's level of disability is described as being on the border between moderate and mild
- Her communication skills are better than those of P and her emotional understanding is quite sophisticated
- Q also has problems with her sight
- Q exhibits challenging behaviour with 'autistic traits'
- Q initially was moved into the home of her former respite carer, but owing to her aggressive outbursts, she was moved into a small specialist residential home with three others
- Q had occasional outbursts of challenging behaviour towards the other three residents and sometimes required physical restraint
- She also showed no wish to go out and did not need to be prevented from doing so, but was accompanied by staff whenever she did
- She attended the same education unit as P
- Q had some social life and more than P
- Q was being given risperidone to control her anxiety

> **Box 7.2** The situation of P (in Cheshire West)
>
> About P in Cheshire West
>
> - P lived with his mother until the age of 37
> - P's mother developed health problems and in November 2009 he was moved under the authority of an order of the Court of Protection to Z House
> - Z House is described as a spacious bungalow, with a cosy and pleasant atmosphere, which P shared with two other residents
> - There are two staff on duty during the day and one waking member overnight
> - P received significant additional one-to-one support to help him leave the house whenever he chose
> - He attended a day centre four days a week and hydrotherapy on the fifth day
> - P also went to a club, pub and the shops and he regularly saw his mother, who lived close to his bungalow
> - He could walk for short distances but needed a wheelchair to go further

of his situation are summarised in Box 7.2. In addition, he had marked communication difficulties; he needed prompts and significant help with activities of daily living and wore incontinence pads. P had the habit of putting pieces of faecally contaminated pads in his mouth and staff had to resort to dressing him in an all-in-one bodysuit to prevent this. He was not prescribed any medication.

In the Court of Protection it was successfully argued that P was deprived of his liberty for a number of reasons, including the following: the requirement for intrusive physical interventions and restraint; the monitoring of every aspect of his life with 'complete and effective control' over his care and movements; and his lack of freedom to leave the premises unescorted.

The local authority appealed the judgment. In the Court of Appeal Lord Justice Munby[64] concluded that P was not deprived of his liberty. In so doing he made the observation that 'because of his disabilities, P is inherently restricted in the kind of life he can lead' and introduced the notion of the 'relevant comparator'. So, when interpreting the 'normality' of a setting, the relevant comparator is: 'an adult of similar age with the same capabilities as X, affected by the same condition or suffering the same inherent mental and physical disabilities and limitations [...] as X'. Although the purpose of the 'relevant comparator' was to introduce an objective assessment into the determination of deprivation, arguably it only added to the complexity and confusion.

The Cheshire West ruling and its implications

In March 2014, the majority verdict in the Supreme Court was that all three appellants were deprived of their liberty. Lady Hale highlighted the key principle that human rights are universal and thereby apply to everyone and that this underpins the UN Convention on the Rights of Persons with Disabilities (UNCRPD). She made it clear that 'what it means to be deprived of liberty must be the same for everyone, whether or not they have physical or mental disabilities'. She stated:

'If it would be a deprivation of my liberty to be obliged to live in a particular place, subject to constant monitoring and control, only allowed out with close supervision, and unable to move away without permission even if such an opportunity became available, then it must also be a deprivation of the liberty of a disabled person. The fact that my living arrangements are comfortable, and indeed make my life as enjoyable as it could possibly be, should make no difference. A gilded cage is still a cage.'[59]

The key phrase used in the Bournewood case[57] and repeated in all cases thereafter was whether the person concerned was subject to 'continuous supervision and control and was not free to leave'. Along with the deprivation being the responsibility of the State, this forms the basis of the 'acid test'. Factors that were not relevant were also set out: the person's compliance or lack of objection, and the relative normality of the placement and the reason or purpose behind it. Also the comparator should in principle be 'a person with unimpaired health and capacity'.

The implications of the Supreme Court ruling in Cheshire West are enormous and hugely change the range of situations in which deprivation of liberty is considered to be occurring. This inevitably means that far more people will require authorisation for deprivation of liberty. Within 6 months of the ruling, there had been a ninefold increase in the number of DoLS applications; 50% of the assessments were not completed within the statutory time frame of 21 days.[65] A tenfold increase in DoLS cases is expected, from 10 184 in 2013–2014 to over 100 000 in 2014–2015, with anticipated costs of meeting the surge in demand to be at least £45 million, excluding legal costs.[66] There are also many who are outside the scope of the DoLS provisions (i.e. not in hospitals or registered care homes) whose deprivation of liberty requires Court of Protection authorisation, for example those in supported living. There will also be those aged 16 and over being cared for in a family home (whether by relatives, foster carers or other arrangements), but with a sufficient degree of State involvement to engage Article 5 of the European Convention on Human Rights and whose deprivation of liberty therefore requires Court of Protection authorisation. In some circumstances there has also been a need to revisit previous decision-making in relation to deprivation of liberty.

Further practical implications are the relative paucity of Best Interests Assessors and medical assessors. Given the large numbers of individuals to whom the ruling will apply, there is a risk that authorising a deprivation of liberty will assume the characteristic of an administrative obligation rather than a protection of the safeguards of vulnerable mentally incapacitated individuals. Furthermore, situations frequently arise in general hospitals where patients are not able to give valid consent to their care or treatment.

Many conditions that result in lack of capacity meet the criteria of a mental disorder under the MHA (e.g. delirium and dementia) and many do not. This is a very common state of affairs. Although the broader provisions of the MCA would formerly cover situations such as these, it is clear from a Court of Protection judgment arising 'post-Cheshire West' that the acid test will be met in acute medical settings.[67] The choice of which Act (MCA or MHA) to use to authorise any deprivation of liberty in these situations is not always straightforward (see below and Chapter 1). What is more, the DoLS process is just too slow to offer protection, given the natural history of many physical conditions that cause impaired decision-making capacity. The DoLS scheme as conceived was simply not intended for most situations arising in general hospitals.

Lord Neuberger, in the Cheshire West judgment,[59] addressed the position of children (he didn't specify the upper age but one must remember that DoLS only apply to people aged 18 and over). He noted that the ordinary family set up will not engage Article 5 because there is no State involvement. However, where a child is looked after by foster parents, it is the State's involvement in placing the child that may engage Article 5 and there may be a deprivation of liberty. There may be some cases where the State is under a positive obligation to end abnormal restrictions on a child's liberty even when these are imposed in a private home. Further to this, the law on consent in children, if not already complex enough, is perhaps now even more demanding as parental authority itself is insufficient to authorise deprivation of liberty for a child who is unable to give their own consent. If the MHA is not available, under certain circumstances a court order may be required. Again, more guidance is required to clarify this difficult area.

After Cheshire West

Further case law has emerged since the Cheshire West judgment that does little to ease the quandaries of health and social care staff in their decision-making in relation to deprivation of liberty. The circumstances of care of a 52-year-old woman in her own home were generally considered to amount to a deprivation of her liberty. The judge disagreed and expressed the following view:

> 'If her family had money and had devised and paid for the very same arrangement this could not be a situation of deprivation of liberty. But because they are devised and paid for by organs of the state they are said so to be, and the whole panoply of authorisation and review required by Article 5 (and its explications) is brought into play. In my opinion this is arbitrary, arguably irrational, and a league away from the intentions of the framers of the Convention'.[68]

The case went to appeal but wasn't heard because both parties agreed that the woman was deprived of her liberty and this was accepted, without a hearing, by the Court of Appeal. That there was no hearing to further clarify the issues was a pity from the point of view of clinicians.

79

The Deprivation of Liberty Safeguards

The Deprivation of Liberty Safeguards (DoLS) are complex and introduced new terminology, roles and procedures. The safeguards cover people who:

▶ are aged 18 or over (under 18s can be deprived of their liberty using the authority of the Children Act 1989)

▶ suffer from mental disorder or learning disability

▶ lack decision-making capacity in relation to their residency in a hospital or care home

▶ need to be, or are being, deprived of their liberty, and

▶ fulfil the qualifying requirements discussed below.

The DoLS cannot be used in respect of people living in their own home, in supported living schemes or in other accommodation not registered as a hospital or care home. The Court of Protection would be required to authorise deprivation of liberty in these settings. Importantly, the deprivation of liberty must be in the individual's own best interests, as defined by the MCA, in order to protect them from harm and ensure that they receive the care they need. Provisions for people deprived of their liberty to challenge their deprivation in the Court of Protection are included. Unlike the requirements of the MHA, individuals with learning disabilities can be subject to the DoLS whether or not their disability is associated with abnormally aggressive or seriously irresponsible conduct.

Note

Many people with learning disabilities live in supported living schemes and although they have tenancy agreements they do not necessarily have capacity. Some were moved from long-stay institutions to supported living and their history of non-convicted but serious offending behaviour means that they are commonly deprived of their liberty.

The 'Managing Authority' of a hospital or care home is responsible for applying for a standard authorisation of deprivation of liberty to the 'Supervisory Body'. In the case of an NHS hospital, the Managing Authority is the NHS body responsible for running the hospital. This is the Trust Board, although responsibility for DoLS may be delegated to Ward/Unit Manager level. In the case of a care home or private hospital, the Managing Authority is the person registered under Part 2 of the Care Standards Act 2000. From 2013, the Supervisory Body is the commissioning local authority for both hospitals (in England) and care homes. Which local authority depends on where the person is 'ordinarily resident'. A person in hospital is ordinarily resident in the local authority area where they are registered with a general practitioner. If a patient is not registered with a general practitioner, then they are ordinarily resident in the area where they usually live.

When a Managing Authority believes that an authorisation is required, because they are depriving, or are about to deprive, a person of their liberty, they must submit the appropriate DoLS standard forms to the Supervisory Body. The Supervisory Body is required to have procedures in place to: respond to requests for standard and emergency authorisations; commission assessments; and, if all the assessments agree, authorise deprivation of liberty.

A standard authorisation must be completed within 21 days. Where deprivation of liberty needs to be authorised in an emergency, the Managing Authority may itself issue an urgent authorisation pending completion of the standard authorisation application process. An urgent authorisation may initially be for a maximum of 7 days, but may be extended by the Supervisory Body for up to a further 7 days in exceptional circumstances.

The Supervisory Body is required to arrange for the following assessments to be undertaken in order to establish whether or not the qualifying requirements are met:

▶ age assessment
▶ mental health assessment
▶ mental capacity assessment
▶ best interests assessment
▶ eligibility assessment
▶ no refusals assessment.

Table 7.1 outlines the questions that must be answered by the assessments and the professionals who are authorised to do so. There is a requirement for a minimum of two assessors, who must record their conclusions on standard forms. A DoL authorisation cannot be issued if any of the qualifying requirements is not met.

Professional roles

The assessment for authorisation involves two professionals: the Mental Health Assessor and the Best Interests Assessor.

▶ The Mental Health Assessor must be a Registered Medical Practitioner either approved under section 12 of the MHA, or with at least 3 years' post-registration experience in the diagnosis or treatment of mental disorder, such as a general practitioner with a special interest. Note that Registered Medical Practitioners who are Approved Clinicians automatically have section 12 approval.

The primary role of the Mental Health Assessor is to ensure that the 'mental health' qualifying requirement is met, i.e. that the person has a mental disorder within the meaning of the MHA. The Mental Health Assessor may also conduct the capacity assessment and, if section 12 approved, the eligibility test. The Mental Health Assessor must not

Table 7.1 Purpose and personnel for the DoLS assessments

Assessment	Question	Who can carry out assessment
Age	Is the person over 18?	Best Interests Assessor (as defined in last row)
No refusals	Would the DoL authorisation conflict with another decision-making authority, e.g. advance decision, lasting power of attorney or Court Appointed Deputy?	Best Interests Assessor (as defined in last row)
Mental capacity	Does the person lack the appropriate decision-making capacity, e.g. to choose whether they should be accommodated in a hospital or care home or receive the recommended treatment?	A Registered Medical Practitioner approved under section 12 of the MHA, or one with special experience in the diagnosis or treatment of mental disorder (must have completed the appropriate training) or the Best Interests Assessor
Mental health	Does the person have a mental disorder within the meaning of the MHA? How is the deprivation of their liberty likely to affect the person's mental health?	Doctor approved under section 12 of the MHA, or with special experience in diagnosis or treatment of mental disorder, e.g. GP with special interest (must have completed appropriate training)
Eligibility	The person would not be eligible for DoL authorisation if: they are or should be detained as a hospital in-patient under the MHA; or the authorisation would be inconsistent with a requirement placed on them under the MHA	Approved Mental Health Professional or section 12 approved doctor
Best interests	Is deprivation of liberty occurring or going to occur? If so, is it in the best interests of the person?	Best Interests Assessor: an Approved Mental Health Professional or other professional, such as a social worker, nurse, occupational therapist or psychologist, with appropriate level of experience and competencies

DoLS, Deprivation of Liberty Safeguards; MHA, Mental Health Act 1983.

conduct the best interests assessment. To become approved you must have completed the standard training for deprivation of liberty Mental Health Assessors.

▶ The Best Interests Assessor (BIA) may be a social worker, nurse, occupational therapist or chartered psychologist who has satisfactorily completed assessor training approved by the Secretary of State.[69]

The Best Interests Assessor plays a central role in the DoLS process comparable to that of the Approved Mental Health Professional (AMHP) in the Mental Health Act assessment process. The Best Interests Assessor must complete the best interests assessment and ensure that the 'age' and 'no refusals' requirements are met, and may make the capacity assessment. If the Best Interests Assessor is also an Approved Mental Health Professional, then they may also conduct the eligibility test. The Best Interests Assessor is therefore required to evaluate the care plan, seek the views of anyone involved in caring for the person, involve the person and support them in the decision-making process, as well as specify any necessary conditions and recommend someone to be appointed as the Relevant Person's Representative (see p. 84). The Best Interests Assessor also receives the reports from the Mental Health Assessor and writes a report to the Supervisory Body indicating whether they support the authorisation of deprivation of liberty and for how long any authorisation should last.

The interface between the MCA and the MHA in relation to deprivation of liberty

We discussed the interface between the MCA and MHA in relation to treatment in Chapter 2. Some patients need additionally to be deprived of their liberty. Which legal framework should then be used?

If the patient doesn't need to be in hospital, i.e. can be cared for and treated (for either physical or mental illness) in a care home, then only the DoLS can authorise the deprivation of liberty. If the patient is to be deprived of their liberty for the assessment or treatment of a physical illness in hospital, then the DoLS is appropriate. The confusion arises if the patient is to be deprived of their liberty in hospital for the assessment or treatment of their mental disorder. There are two possible schemes: the MCA with DoLS or the MHA. The choice as to which to use is determined by Schedule 1A of the MCA. This isn't easy.

Points to consider

▶ Does the patient come within the broad framework for use of the MCA? Is the patient over 18 years of age, do they lack capacity, is the detention in their best interests, and if they are being deprived of their liberty in order to give a particular medical treatment, is there no valid and applicable advance refusal of that treatment or an objection by the patient's welfare attorney? If the answer to any of these is negative, the DoLS cannot be used.

▶ Is the patient currently detained under the MHA? If so, the DoLS cannot be used.

▶ Is the patient subject to the MHA but not currently detained (e.g. is the person on a Community Treatment Order)? If so and the patient needs to be deprived of their liberty in a care home, i.e. they don't need to be in hospital, then the DoLS can be used. But if the patient needs to have medical treatment to which they are objecting or resisting, then this treatment cannot be given under the MCA and the patient would need to be recalled to hospital under the MHA.

▶ If the patient is informal and requires deprivation of liberty for the assessment or treatment of mental disorder, then the MHA must be used if the patient has capacity and is refusing or lacks capacity and is resisting. But if the patient lacks capacity in relation to the decision to be in hospital and receive treatment for their mental disorder, but is fully compliant, then the MCA with DoLS is the appropriate legal framework.

Note

Particular cases may require legal advice and, rarely, the intervention of the Court of Protection or the High Court. For example, if a patient is detained in hospital under the MHA and then requires treatment for an unrelated physical illness which, independently, would require the patient to be deprived of their liberty, only the court can authorise this.[70]

Granting of DoLS authorisation

The Supervisory Body cannot give authorisation unless all the assessments are supportive. If authorisation is granted, the Supervisory Body must specify the duration of the authorisation, which cannot exceed 12 months and cannot be longer than the recommendation of the Best Interests Assessor. The Supervisory Body may attach conditions to the authorisation, and the Managing Authority is obliged to comply with these. Certain people must receive a copy of the authorisation, specifically the Managing Authority, the person themselves (the Relevant Person), any Independent Mental Capacity Advocate involved, any person consulted by the Best Interests Assessor and named in their report, along with the Relevant Person's Representative. The Supervisory Body can be required to review the authorisation at any time at the request of the person, their representative or any Independent Mental Capacity Advocate representing them. A review may also be initiated if there has been a significant change in the person's circumstances and, if appropriate, the authorisation revoked before it expires.

The Relevant Person's Representative

The Relevant Person's Representative is required to maintain contact with the person, represent and support them through the DoLS procedure and, if appropriate, trigger review or application to the Court of Protection. There are restrictions on who may be appointed, but in general the individual must be 18 or over, willing to be appointed and able to keep in contact. In many cases, the representative is a close family member, carer or friend. In addition to the Relevant Person's Representative, the Managing Authority must notify the Supervisory Body when it requests an authorisation if there is no one appropriate to consult about the person's best interests other than paid carers. The Supervisory Body must then instruct an Independent Mental Capacity Advocate to represent the person (see Chapter 6).

The recent report of the Select Committee on the MCA suggested that the Relevant Person's Representative appointment process needs to be improved so that the right person gets the job and, moreover, is listened to.[31]

The DoLS interface with safeguarding adults procedures

'Safeguarding adults procedures' refer to the local, multi-agency response made when an adult's independence or well-being are at risk because of abuse or neglect. These safeguarding processes may intersect with DoLS provisions for a number of reasons. For example, it might be necessary to raise a safeguarding alert if the care plan of a Managing Authority is neglectful or abusive, or a Supervisory Body declines to authorise a deprivation of liberty but the Managing Authority proceeds with the deprivation anyway. Alternatively, a Managing Authority might be asked to make a DoLS application if an unlawful deprivation of liberty is identified during the safeguarding adults process.

The DoLS procedures are frequently invoked when there is a conflict of opinion, for example when a decision to admit a patient to a care home is opposed by relatives and/or carers. There may be circumstances in which there are significant concerns for the safety of a person if discharged, but DoLS should not be used to resolve the matter. Equally, the DoLS process should not be used as a means by which a public authority gets its own way at the expense of an individual's best interests. In either of these circumstances a decision of the Court of Protection may be necessary. A particularly salient case in this respect is that of Mr Steven Neary, who has autism. His father spent nearly a year in dispute with the local authority of Hillingdon, which was preventing Mr Neary's return home after what his father had intended to be a few days of respite care. The local authority was criticised on a number of counts, most importantly that it had granted one urgent DoLS authorisation and three standard DoLS authorisations without conducting an effective review of Mr Neary's best interests. It was concluded that Mr Neary had been unlawfully deprived of his liberty.[71]

There is considerable further detail in relation to the DoLS process, but the most salient features may be summarised as follows.

Review

It is important that the circumstances of the person who is deprived of their liberty remain under review and that the care plan developed by the Managing Authority corresponds to any change in their situation. The Supervisory Body is authorised to conduct a review at any time, but the law requires a review if one is requested by the person themselves or their representative or the Managing Authority. It may be that the person no longer meets the qualifying requirements or that the threshold and criteria for detention under the MHA are met. Furthermore, the reasons for the authorisation may have changed, or the conditions of the authorisation may need to be amended. Once a review has been instigated, the Supervisory Body has the power to vary specific conditions attached to the authorisation or to order a full reassessment. The review process can have various outcomes. It may lead to the authorisation being continued in the same form or with amendments or, if the qualifying requirements are no longer met, to its termination or suspension (for up to 28 days). Suspension may be appropriate if the person is newly detained under the MHA. The DoLS authorisation may be reactivated if the Managing Authority notifies the Supervisory Body that the person has again become eligible in that time period; otherwise the authorisation is terminated.

Renewal

When the period of a standard authorisation ends, the authority to deprive someone of their liberty terminates. If the Managing Authority considers that the person must continue to be deprived of their liberty, a further standard authorisation beginning after the expiry of the existing authorisation must be requested and then commissioned by the Supervisory Body. There is no extension. A new DoLS authorisation is required.

Notification of unauthorised deprivation of liberty

If the person, or a significant other such as a relative, carer, friend or inspecting body, thinks that the person is being deprived of their liberty without appropriate authorisation, they should draw this to the attention of the Managing Authority, who should respond within a reasonable time. The DoLS Code of Practice[3] indicates that this should be within 24 hours. If it is not possible to resolve the issue, the Managing Authority should apply for a standard authorisation. If this process is not enacted, the concerned person should contact the Supervisory Body, which should arrange a preliminary assessment to decide whether the person is deprived of their liberty, and if so, to instruct the Managing Authority to request a standard authorisation. The assessment might find that the person is not being deprived of their liberty or that they are either lawfully or unlawfully so deprived.

Note

If a patient dies while detained under the DoLS, the death must be reported to the Coroner.[69]

Court of Protection

For disputes that cannot be otherwise resolved, the Court of Protection may be asked to declare on a number of issues. The Court may have to resolve challenges to the lawfulness of authorisations under the DoLS scheme or to the details of the authorisations. The Court has the power, among other things, to decide on how long an authorisation is to be in force, the purpose for which it is given and the conditions to which the person is subject. The Court may also issue an order to terminate or vary an authorisation or direct the Supervisory Body to do so.

The Regulations

The Mental Capacity DoLS Regulations,[72] together with the MCA itself, stipulate the eligibility requirements for people who carry out the assessments. By identifying conflicts of interest, they provide some guidance for Supervisory Bodies on selecting individuals to carry out assessments. The regulations specify the information, if available, that the Managing Authority must include in a request for a standard authorisation. Where there is dispute, the regulations resolve the question of who should act as the Supervisory Body until the question of ordinary residence is determined. Finally, there is also provision to effect a change in Supervisory Body.

Conclusions

Since their introduction, the DoLS provisions have been criticised for being overly complex and excessively bureaucratic. Often it appears that staff do not understand them; that there is confusion over the differences between the powers of the Mental Health Act and DoLS and the terminology of the European Convention on Human Rights lacks clarity. A House of Lords Select Committee[31] described DoLS as 'not fit for purpose' and called for them to be replaced with something that is much more in keeping with the character of the Mental Capacity Act. It recommended that the new system should extend to cover people in supported living arrangements. Soon after the Select Committee reported, the Supreme Court judgment in Cheshire West[59] was to vastly increase the number of people who were considered to be deprived of their liberty. Despite this, it is important to recognise that just being obliged to live in any particular place or geographical area may not in itself necessarily amount to deprivation of liberty. A combination of factors may be operating that must be considered together and there may be difficulty in classification of borderline cases. However, the threshold is low.

Even with the ruling of the Supreme Court in Cheshire West, there is still a long way to go before we see how the legal state of affairs eventually resolves. The Select Committee recommended that the Law Commission considers how deprivation of liberty should be authorised and supervised in hospitals, care homes and community settings where it is possible that Article 5 rights would otherwise be infringed. Meanwhile, attempts to streamline the processes of the Court of Protection[73,74] to cope with the anticipated large increase in applications to the Court have already been appealed; further cases may well be referred to the Supreme Court. People continue to agonise over the wording of the acid test: what really amounts to 'complete and effective control' and when is someone truly 'free to leave'? The important issue for practitioners will be the effect on the person and whether carers are effectively deciding on all aspects of daily life, and not necessarily that the person is being supervised for every minute of the day. Lady Hale's position was to 'err on the side of caution',[59] which is perhaps the best advice that can be offered until the Law Commission makes its report and further changes to the law, if any, are implemented.

CHAPTER 8

The Court of Protection, clinically relevant judgments from the courts and writing reports

The Court of Protection (CoP) deals with decision-making on health and welfare and on property and affairs. The Court is a superior court of record (a court in which proceedings are recorded and transcripts made available) and is assisted by the activity of the Office of the Public Guardian (OPG) and Court of Protection Visitors. The Court of Protection and Office of the Public Guardian work together but have different roles. Essentially, the Court of Protection makes the decisions and the Office of the Public Guardian sorts out the administration. The Court hears approximately 23 000 cases every year.[75]

The Office of the Public Guardian coordinates a panel of Court of Protection Visitors (section 61 of the MCA).

There are two sorts of Court of Protection Visitor:

▶ General Visitors (not medically qualified, but with experience in the field of mental incapacity)

▶ Special Visitors (medically qualified, with experience in the field of mental incapacity).

General Visitors gather information about the person's welfare or running of their estate and have rights to obtain information and interview the person in private. The role of visitors is especially important if there are no relatives or friends to act as a deputy and report problems to the court.

Special Visitors may undertake a private medical, psychiatric or psychological assessment of the person's capacity and condition in order to produce a report for the court.

The purpose of the Visitors' reports is to help the Public Guardian to supervise deputies and, where necessary, investigate concerns about the actions of deputies or attorneys. The reports also help the Court of Protection to make decisions.

If other authorities are unable to agree on the best interests of a person who lacks capacity, then the Court of Protection will make the decision. In cases where there is uncertainty about whether or not someone can make their own decision about a specific issue, the Court of Protection can also determine whether or not the person lacks capacity to make the decision.

For personal welfare issues, the Court of Protection would be involved only if the parties are unable to agree what is in the person's best interests.

The judge for each case will decide whether the media should be admitted. If the media are allowed entry, the judge determines what can be reported. The person's identity is usually protected by the use of a single letter or set of initials.

The functions of the Court of Protection

The functions of the Court of Protection include:

▶ making final decisions over the health, welfare and financial affairs of people who lack capacity to make the decisions for themselves
▶ appointing a deputy to make a decision or manage the personal welfare or property and affairs on the person's behalf, and:
  ▶ ensuring that the deputy acts correctly
  ▶ removing the deputy if they do not act correctly
▶ determining issues relating to lasting powers of attorney
▶ making declarations on:
  ▶ whether the person has capacity to make a particular decision
  ▶ whether an act done, or proposed to be done, in relation to the person is lawful
▶ making decisions about:
  ▶ where the person can live
  ▶ with whom the person can have contact
  ▶ giving, or refusing, consent to the commencing or continuing of medical treatment
  ▶ directing that an individual responsible for the person's healthcare allows a different individual to take over that responsibility.

In relation to property and affairs, the Court has jurisdiction over:

▶ the control and management of the person's property
▶ the sale, exchange, charging, gift or other disposition of the person's property
▶ the acquisition of property in the person's name or on the person's behalf
▶ the carrying on of any profession, trade or business on the person's behalf
▶ the taking of a decision that will have the effect of dissolving a partnership of which the person is a member
▶ the carrying out of any contract entered into by the person

- ▶ the discharge of the person's debts and of any of the person's obligations, whether legally enforceable or not
- ▶ the settlement of any of the person's property, whether for the person's benefit or for the benefit of others
- ▶ the execution for the person of a will
- ▶ the exercise of any power (including a power to consent) vested in the person whether beneficially or as trustee or otherwise
- ▶ the conduct of legal proceedings in the person's name or on the person's behalf.

The deputies appointed by the court may deal with property and affairs or health and welfare. For 'one-off' decisions related to health and welfare (e.g. a surgical procedure or accommodation placement) the Court may make a single ruling. For complex cases, where there may be a series of linked decisions or a continuing requirement for decision-making, the Court may appoint a deputy. The Court regards delegation of these duties as a very serious matter and will only do so where important and necessary acts cannot be carried out without the Court's authority or there is no other way of settling the matter in the best interests of the person concerned.

Who can be a Court Appointed Deputy?

Deputies must be at least 18 years of age and must possess the necessary knowledge and skills to act in the relevant person's best interests for those matters for which they have decision-making authority. Typically, a Court Appointed Deputy would be a trusted family member or an officer of the local authority.

If there is a history of disputes within the family (e.g. regarding where the person should live or whether or not they should receive medical treatment), disagreement between family members and professionals, or the person might be at risk if left in the family's care, the Court may place limitations on the decisions that can be made and the duration of the authority.

It is important to note that there is a procedure for appealing against a Court of Protection decision.[76]

What kinds of health and welfare situations go to the Court of Protection?

Cases that go to the Court of Protection tend to involve complex situations regarding people with learning disabilities or mental health problems who lack capacity to make the relevant decisions. They commonly relate to safeguarding of adults, for example:

- disputes between a person or their relatives and local authorities over issues of residence
- allegations of physical or financial abuse by a spouse or relative
- applications to use a gastrostomy ('PEG') tube, against the family's wishes, to feed someone with a severe learning disability whose physical condition is deteriorating
- allegations of threats of or actual violence by parents against someone with learning disabilities and mental illness who is still living at home
- return from prison of a convicted sex offender to a household in which a vulnerable adult is living
- pregnancy in a woman with a learning disability that is likely to cause serious harm owing to deteriorating mental illness
- a vulnerable adult seriously affected by continuing disputes between estranged parents
- in cases of abuse, resolving issues of residency and contact with abusive family.

Contacting the Court

Although hearings may be held in regional courts, all applications relating to people who lack capacity to make specific decisions must be made via the Court of Protection's central registry in Archway, north London. The London registry deals with urgent interim directions and, if appropriate, refers cases to regional centres for a hearing. Specific groups of people have a right to apply to the Court. These include the person themselves; attorneys under a lasting power of attorney to which the decision relates; the Relevant Person's Representative (or Independent Mental Capacity Advocate) for someone subject to a DoLS authorisation (see Chapter 7); the Official Solicitor; and the Public Guardian. Other people concerned with the welfare of the person need to get permission from the Court to make an application. The Court of Protection Rules relating to permission to make an application are, at the time of writing, under review.

Note

Where a person lacks litigation capacity, a Litigation Friend is appointed by the Court to carry on the proceedings on their behalf. The Official Solicitor has a number of functions, including acting as Litigation Friend for people unable to represent themselves and who have no other suitable person or agency able or willing to act for them. The Office of the Official Solicitor is part of the Ministry of Justice.

What do I do if a patient of mine goes to the Court of Protection?

Most clinicians will be happy to navigate their career without being involved in any court proceedings. Unfortunately, you may not always have the choice. A patient under your care may be involved in Court of Protection proceedings and this might necessitate your participation. This can arise in any clinical setting, including obstetric care, surgery and cancer treatment. If it does, what should you do? How do you prepare for the proceedings, which may or may not require your attendance at Court, and ensure that you survive the ordeal? Like any situation, good preparation and knowledge are likely to make the experience less stressful.

Although not always predictable, the first hurdle may be recognising that a situation will require a Court of Protection decision. For example, it might involve one of the decisions that has special protections under the MCA (see Decisions outside the scope of section 5, pp. 22–23 above). Or attempts to resolve a dispute regarding a person's capacity or best interests using measures such as mediation or obtaining a second opinion (see Chapter 4) might have failed. Once you have recognised that the Court might have to be involved, it may be wise to discuss the case with senior managers in your organisation, with a view to seeking legal advice. Most clinicians are not familiar with applications to the Court of Protection or other Court procedures and rules and they require guidance. If the Court needs to make a decision, then early identification of the case is essential in order that the appropriate information can be garnered and so that the necessary agencies and representatives are notified.

It may be wise to review the person's capacity assessments and ensure that detailed and reasoned assessments in relation to the relevant decisions are documented. It can be relatively straightforward to challenge a capacity assessment on the basis of fluctuation, so be mindful of this and keep capacity under review.

The practice and processes of the Court of Protection are relatively complex and beyond the scope of this text, but the following gives a flavour of some of the available options.

The Court process

The first consideration of the Court will be the appropriateness of the application to the Court, whether alternative remedies can be applied and whether permission to make an application needs to be sought. The Court may then order a directions hearing with a view to identifying the relevant issues and what evidence needs to be put before the Court and by whom. Depending on the circumstances, the judge may at this point need to make interim declarations in relation to capacity or best interests pending consideration of further evidence.

As treating clinician, you may be asked for a report or witness statement. The request will probably come through a lawyer. Ensure that you have it in writing and that it confirms whether (and by when) they need a report, whether and when you should attend court and how long it is likely to take. Ask what the issues are in the case and why you are being asked to give evidence. Depending on the circumstances, the Court may direct an independent expert (or experts) to complete assessments and reports.

We discuss the formalities of report writing in the next section. Our more general advice when writing any report or witness statement is as follows. Stick to the facts and what you know, and be clear about what is your opinion or views and what are matters of fact. Make sure you only disclose information that is relevant to the case. The Court may make an order for general disclosure (any documents to support the case) or specific disclosure (a particular document or documents), but sometimes you will need to use your professional judgement to decide what information is appropriate and relevant to be shared. Given that you may be involved in implementation of any intervention or care plan following the judgment, you may be asked for your views about how this is best undertaken.

Many welfare applications are resolved without the need for a final hearing in Court. Alternative ways are found of settling the dispute, perhaps a multidisciplinary meeting with the relevant parties or more formal mediations.

If, after submitting a report or statement, you are required to attend Court, ask whether there is anything that your original statement/report did not address and whether you can submit an addendum report/statement to save you attending Court. A witness summons is an order summonsing you to Court and demonstrates that the Court considers it mandatory that you attend.

If you are asked to attend Court to provide your evidence orally you can be questioned about your statement or report, but may be allowed to expand on it if something has recently changed. Before going to Court, make sure you are fully acquainted with the patient and their story. Read all the relevant notes and remind yourself of the case. If possible, see the patient again, particularly if you have not assessed them for a while, and make sure that you are completely up to date with the current situation. Reassess their capacity for specific decisions if the Court is likely to ask your opinion on this.

Allow yourself plenty of time to get to Court – you don't want to arrive feeling rushed and flustered. Make sure you know the correct date, time and location and how to get there. Also make sure you have completed everything that the Court asked of you in preparation, including sending the requested documents to the Court, and that you have all the documents that you want to use at the hearing.

Court of Protection cases are usually heard in private in a court room or a judge's room. The proceedings are recorded. When giving your evidence, take your time and speak clearly and slowly. If you don't understand or can't hear the question, ask for it to be repeated. If you are not sure of the answer, say so. If the question is outside of your area of expertise, say so.

Even though proceedings in the Court of Protection are said to be more informal and inquisitorial than formal and adversarial, they can still be very stressful. Good luck!

How to write reports for the Court of Protection

Solicitors' instructions regarding reports for the Court of Protection will be lengthy but comprehensive. For psychiatrists, the issue is usually that of capacity; for others, it may be best interests in relation to treatment alternatives. Depending on the complexity and nature of the case, it may be necessary to assess a person's capacity in relation to number of different matters. Health and welfare cases do not necessarily involve considerations about treatment. For example, the case might relate to capacity to consent to sexual intercourse or marriage, or to make decisions regarding accommodation or contact with relatives.

The request and the assessments

The request may include a series of capacity assessments rather than one specific assessment. For example, the instructions regarding a request for sterilisation of a woman with learning disabilities might ask:

- whether she has the capacity to:
  - consent to sexual relations
  - consent to medical and surgical contraception
  - consent to sterilisation, and
  - litigate in these proceedings
- what the likely impact of sterilisation (including tubal ligation) would be on her mental health
- how other issues arising from the proposed treatment and care plan might affect her best interests.

A request for an assessment is likely to be accompanied by a profusion of notes, including legal documents and medical records. The issue of capacity is likely to be complex – if it were straightforward, it would already have been established and either the person would make their own decision or a best interests decision would be made. Therefore, a good psychiatric interview and report, including background information, is likely to be relevant even if, at first glance, this might appear not to be the case. A report regarding capacity requires much more than a quick assessment of that specific issue, as without the relevant background information the assessment is unlikely to be accurate or helpful.

A person's ability to make a decision can be affected by the immediate situation. For example, at interview the person may be able to provide appropriate responses about decision-making, but these might not be congruent with past behaviour or opinions. Someone able to express what they would do in a certain situation when asked in a moment of calm might lose that ability when called upon to decide in the face of pressure from others, vulnerability, anxiety or inability to assimilate the information at the time. Past opinions and wishes are extremely important, as is the possibility that capacity might be acquired or regained in the future: both factors might lead to a different conclusion about current capacity.

The person's voluntariness (whether they are making a decision freely, without force, coercion or manipulation) should be considered in the assessment. During the examination, try to avoid leading the patient into acquiescence: for example, use open questions, break questions down into short, easily understandable parts and avoid leading questions. Try to make the person feel comfortable with the interview setting and with you.[77]

Owing to the complexity of Court of Protection cases and the possibility that capacity might be acquired with time and education, there are few occasions where one report is sufficient – perhaps to determine capacity about a single event such as surgery. More often, following the initial recommendations, update reports are required to assess how the case is progressing.

Format of reports

There is no set format. Here are a few personal thoughts based on feedback and experience.

▶ Begin the report with your relevant qualifications and experience. Include an abridged version of your most up-to-date CV, showing relevant current and past positions and qualifications, and previous experience of report writing. State who has instructed you and why, who you interviewed/examined as part of the process and how long each interview took. Describe clearly any telephone interviews you had and make specific notes of any written records that you have seen.

▶ End with a conclusion, which should state your views with regard to the person's capacity, and any recommendations about management and facilitation to enable them to gain capacity, if relevant.

▶ After the conclusion, insert a declaration outlining an understanding of your duty to the Court, for example: 'I understand that my overriding duty is to the Court. This duty includes providing written reports and giving oral evidence. I know of no conflict of interest. In preparing this report I have endeavoured to be both accurate and complete. I have shown the sources of all the information I have used. I believe that the facts I have stated in this report are true and the opinions I have expressed are correct'.

► After the declaration, you must sign and date the report.

A typical report might also include the following.

► A psychiatric assessment, including a section on the capacity assessment. If multiple requests for capacity assessment on different issues are made, it is important to address these one at a time, including evidence in each assessment regarding how your conclusion was reached. The person's verbatim responses to questions can be helpful here.

► A description of the degree of disability and information about the cause, for example learning disability, dementia or head injury. As appropriate, make a note of:

  ► specific syndromes associated with learning disability and any known facets affecting specific intellectual processes

  ► IQ test scores

  ► social functioning (scores on adaptive behaviour scales) and daily living skills (what the person can do).

This information would not by itself be determinative but would provide a basis for further assessment (equivalent to the status approach).

► Consideration of whether capacity may be gained in the future, and if so, how. The idea of facilitation is now widely accepted and no longer thought of as 'cheating'. Could capacity be achieved with education, facilitation and development? The nature of developmental delay may mean that someone with a learning disability might not reach their full intellectual capacity until their late 20s. This would affect the assessment of any ability to learn about aspects not currently understood.

► A description of communication skills. The MCA specifically states that it doesn't matter how capacity is communicated as long as it is, but information about how the person is able to interact during assessment is valuable. It is generally assumed that, unless stated, an adult will be able to communicate with another adult in their own language. Does this person have any verbal speech (give verbatim examples)? Do they have non-verbal speech (provide specific examples of how they communicate non-verbally)? Can they understand simple instructions (one-stage, two-stage, three-stage, etc.)? What is the general level of understanding (again, provide verbatim examples of questions and answers if appropriate)?

► An opinion on whether the person understands what the decision in question entails. Information specifically relevant to the decision might include an understanding of the permanency of a procedure, any alternatives, potential benefits and possible side-effects or health risks (mental and physical). This information needs to be given to the person in an understandable format and the person's response to the information and their ability to understand it need to be included in the report.

97

▶ An assessment of the person's voluntariness. Is the person communicating their own decision or displaying acquiescence or disempowerment because of their reduced cognitive ability and social position?

Note

The Mental Capacity Act suggests that the assessment of capacity should be 'facilitated', i.e. the assessors should ensure that the explanation and information the person needs to make the decision are given in a way that makes the task as easy as possible for the person being assessed. For example, assessors might use simple language, pictures or visual aids, or provide the information in small chunks over repeated sessions. If the person is unable to understand the information needed to make their own decision when it is first presented to them, this may be because the manner in which the information was provided is the problem (rather than the person's mental capacity). This needs to be considered and the material re-presented in a way that will help the person being assessed.

The courts in relation to clinical decision-making

The following section deals with clinically relevant issues that have been addressed in the courts, mostly, but not exclusively, in the Court of Protection. The topics have been selected because they are frankly confusing (capacity and sexual relations); because special rules apply (withdrawal of artificial nutrition and hydration and other serious medical decisions); because they often lead to complaints ('do not attempt cardiopulmonary resuscitation' (DNACPR) decisions and the use of antipsychotics in dementia); or for general interest as the cases have been so emotive and controversial (anorexia nervosa).

Capacity to consent to sexual relations

The Court of Protection's approaches to cases involving capacity to give sexual consent have propagated uncertainty and continue to baffle clinicians in their day-to-day work. Community learning disability teams are often faced with complex situations involving the sexual lives of people with learning disabilities that require judgements about when a situation becomes safeguarding a vulnerable adult and when it is allowing individuals to live the 'normal' lives they often crave. It is a very knotty area and, arguably, the tension between these competing issues may be a barrier to successful prosecution of sexual offences. It has been reported that research by Professor Betsy Stanko looking at the Metropolitan Police Force's investigation of rape supports anecdotal clinical experience that people with learning disabilities who report sexual assault are 67% less likely to have their cases referred to the police for prosecution and that people with mental health problems are 40% less likely.[78]

► The case law, as so often, is difficult and at times contradictory and, for many readers, it will not feel particularly intuitive or readily applicable in day-to-day situations. The main point of contention is whether the person's understanding needs only to be about the sexual act or must also include information about the other person. What seems to be clear is that they need to understand the nature and character of the act, its mechanics and health risks, and the risk (but not the implications) of pregnancy. The ability to understand the emotional and moral aspects of sex have been both included and dismissed as irrelevant by the courts. It is clear that the test of capacity to consent to sexual relations is rather general, and although it remains essential to have the ability to use or weigh information, this is required at a low level. Although the rulings in Table 8.1 clarify the relatively low threshold for the test of sexual capacity and clearly permit sexual freedoms, they are of little practical utility in untangling relatively common cases that arise where sexual exploitation may be occurring. Given the complexity of the legal situation, unless one is confident in applying the test for sexual capacity in practice, it may be advisable to seek advice from someone who is if the situation arises.

Decisions related to end of life

The MCA places decisions relating to 'life-sustaining treatment' within special protections. Life-sustaining treatment is defined in the Act as 'treatment which in the view of a person providing health care for the person concerned is necessary to sustain life'. A treatment is life sustaining because the treating healthcare professional judges it to be so, not because of some unique property inherent in it. The definition is worded so that, as new treatments evolve, they may be included under it without redrafting of the law. The MCA (section 4(5)) makes clear that 'Where the determination relates to life-sustaining treatment [the decision maker] must not, in considering whether the treatment is in the best interests of the person concerned, be motivated by a desire to bring about his death'. The intent of this provision is to demonstrate beyond doubt that the law does not allow euthanasia through withholding or withdrawing life-sustaining treatment. This does not prevent a clinician prescribing a treatment, for example pain relief, that is in the best interests of the patient but can also shorten life. It is also lawful not to prescribe and to discontinue treatment, where the treatment may cause, rather than relieve, suffering or be too burdensome for the patient to bear.

Note

A treatment, or its withholding, must not be for the purpose of ending the patient's life.

Table 8.1 Cases relating to consent to sexual relations

Case	Judgment
X City Council v MB[79]	Justice Munby defined the test for sexual capacity as follows: a person needs to 'understand the nature and the character of the act' and their 'knowledge and understanding does not need to be complete or sophisticated [...] it is enough that [they have] sufficient rudimentary knowledge of what the act comprises and of its sexual nature'.
MM v Local Authority X[80]	Justice Munby explained that capacity to consent to sexual relations was act specific, not person specific, saying that: 'A woman either has capacity, for example, to consent to "normal" penetrative vaginal intercourse, or she does not. It is difficult to see how it can sensibly be said that she has capacity to consent to a particular sexual act with Y whilst at the same time lacking capacity to consent to precisely the same sexual act with Z'. Both this judgment and *X City Council v MB* set a very low threshold for having sexual capacity.
R v C[81]	*R v C* was a criminal case in the Supreme Court. Both the lower and higher courts agreed that the tests should be the same in both criminal and civil contexts. However, Lady Hale disagreed with the preceding judgments[79,80] and ruled that capacity to consent to a sexual relationship is person and situation specific: 'One does not consent to sex in general'.
D County Council v LS[82]	In addition to 'understanding', Justice Wood held that there was the added requirement that the individual be able to retain and weigh the relevant information in the balance and should not be prevented from using or weighing the information because of other factors, such as 'irrational fear'.
D Borough Council v AB[83]	Justice Mostyn held that the capacity to consent to sex remains act specific and requires an understanding and awareness: (a) of the mechanics of the act; (b) that there are health risks involved, particularly the acquisition of sexually transmitted and sexually transmissible infections; and (c) that sex between a man and a woman may result in the woman becoming pregnant.
A Local Authority v H[84]	H demonstrated highly sexualised behaviours. Justice Hedley held that sex has 'not just a physical but an emotional and moral component as well'. He concluded that the relevant information 'should suffice if a person understands that sexual relations may lead to significant ill-health and that those risks can be reduced by precautions like a condom'. He deliberated the moral and emotional aspects of sex, but concluded that a workable test including moral and emotional factors is not possible.

continued

Table 8.1 *continued*

Case	Judgment
A Local Authority v TZ[85]	The Court of Protection took the act-specific approach again. The case involved a long-standing relationship and Justice Baker considered the act-specific approach 'more consistent with respect for autonomy in matters of private life, particularly in the context of the statutory provisions of the MCA and specifically the presumption of capacity and the obligation to take all practical steps to enable a person to make a decision. To require the issue of capacity to be considered in respect of every person with whom TZ contemplated sexual relations would not only be impracticable but would also constitute a great intrusion into his private life'.
IM v LM and Others[86]	The Court of Appeal considered the test of capacity to consent to sexual relations. LM had a history of drug and alcohol misuse and had suffered a brain injury following a cardiac arrest. It was held that LM lacked capacity to make decisions concerning residence, care and contact with others, but had capacity to make decisions about whether or not to have sexual relations. It was confirmed that the test for capacity to consent to sexual relations is general and issue specific, rather than person or event specific, and that this approach was not at odds with the view of Lady Hale in *R v C*.[81]

In cases of terminal illness or in serious illness where further treatment is futile, the clinician and other health workers involved in making decisions about treatment will be able to follow the Code of Practice[2] best interests checklist to determine an appropriate course of action. This applies to the withholding or withdrawal of treatment as well as the use of treatments, such as pain relief or sedation, that may relieve symptoms but hasten death. Effective and sensitive communication is, of course, a hallmark of good practice in end-of-life care. In the case of patients who are unable to participate in the decisions, this practice also protects the practitioners involved in the decision-making.

Note

If there is doubt or unresolved disagreement, it may be necessary to obtain the authority of the court.

Withdrawal of artificial nutrition and hydration and other serious medical decisions

For patients in a persistent vegetative state or a minimally conscious state whose life is sustained by artificial nutrition and hydration, there must be a referral to the Court of Protection for authority to withdraw artificial nutrition and hydration if withdrawal may lead to death. Other decisions listed as requiring a decision of the Court are:

▶ cases involving organ or bone marrow donation by a person who lacks capacity to consent to it (because of the need to determine that it is in the person's best interests even though they will not benefit directly and may suffer pain from the procedure – see below)

▶ cases involving the proposed non-therapeutic sterilisation of a person who lacks capacity to consent to this (e.g. for the purpose of contraception)

▶ all other cases where there is a doubt or dispute about whether a particular treatment will be in a person's best interests (an example given in the MCA Code of Practice (para. 19) is innovative treatments for variant Creutzfeldt–Jakob disease).

Case law in relation to bone marrow and organ donation illustrates how wide the definition of best interests may be. Ms Y was 25 years old and had learning and physical disabilities and epilepsy.[87] She was visited regularly in her care home by her mother and her 36-year-old sister, Ms P. Ms P had the blood condition myelodysplasia, which was transforming into leukaemia, and she was advised that a bone marrow transplant might help her. Ms Y could not consent to bone marrow testing and Ms P sought a declaration that it would be lawful for her sister to undergo tests and donate bone marrow to her. It was held that testing and donation would be in Ms Y's best interests because the consequences for Ms Y of Ms P's death would be that she would lose the visits from Ms P and also see less of her mother, who would have to devote more time to looking after Ms P's child.

In relation to end-of-life decisions and withdrawal of artificial nutrition and hydration, it is difficult to do justice to this complex, tragic and often highly emotionally charged area of case law in such limited space. The following section describes some of the important cases if only to draw the reader's attention to the considerations before the courts and thereby the general principles that are applied.

Mr Tony Bland was in a persistent vegetative state (PVS) following the Hillsborough football stadium disaster. He was kept alive by artificial nutrition and hydration. The Court or Protection determined that this was medical treatment, not basic care, and could be withdrawn as it was not in Mr Bland's best interests. Sir Thomas Bingham, in his judgment said: 'Mere prolongation of life of a PVS patient [...] with no prospect of recovery [...] is not necessarily in his best interests'.[88]

This view was reiterated and expanded by Justice Ryder in the case of CW, also in a persistent vegetative state: 'for patients in a permanent vegetative state where treatment is futile, overly burdensome or intolerable for the patient or where there is no prospect of recovery, it may be in the best interests of the patient to withdraw or withhold treatment and/or to give palliative care that might incidentally shorten life'.[89]

The situation of Miss B was very different. She was paralysed from the neck down and wished the mechanical ventilation that was keeping her alive switched off. In her judgment, Dame Elizabeth Butler-Sloss reinforced the primacy of patient autonomy by her ruling that Miss B had the 'necessary mental capacity to give consent or to refuse', indeed that continuing to treat her would be unlawful.[16]

More recently, *Aintree v James*[90] was the first case under the MCA to appear before the Supreme Court. The patient, Mr James, a professional guitarist, survived cancer surgery in 2001 but in 2012 was admitted to hospital with a problem with his stoma. He suffered an infection and other complications, resulting in his needing to be placed on a ventilator. He then had a stroke, which left him with right-sided weakness and contracture of his legs, and a cardiac arrest (requiring 6 minutes of advanced cardio-pulmonary resuscitation). He had recurring infections, leading to septic shock and multiple organ failure. He was fitted with a tracheostomy, being completely dependent on artificial ventilation, and received artificial feeding and nutrition. He was not able make decisions about his medical treatment. The view of the clinical team was that it would not be in Mr James's best interests to receive these treatments. His family disagreed, indicating that he was able to recognise his wife and son, that he still enjoyed life, he had battled cancer and had survived the serious challenges of the current admission.

The decision to withhold treatment was initially refused by the Court of Protection, overturned by the Court of Appeal, and although Mr James died shortly after this, his family continued with an appeal to the Supreme Court. In her judgment,[90] Lady Hale gave some helpful reminders about the law governing medical decision-making, paraphrased as follows.

▶ The MCA has no more decision-making powers then a capacitous patient would have. Therefore the starting point is to consider what treatment options would be available to the patient if they had capacity.

▶ A doctor cannot be forced to administer treatment that is not clinically indicated. Therefore families cannot insist on a treatment that is not clinically indicated, even if the patient would have requested it.

▶ The authority to treat comes from valid consent in the case of a capacitous patient, and in the case of an incapacitous patient, is lawful only if it is in their best interests.

▶ Therefore the court must focus on whether it is in the best interests of the patient to receive the proposed treatment rather than in their best interests to withdraw or withhold it.

Turning to best interests, Lady Hale said :

'The purpose of the best interests test is to consider matters from the patient's point of view. That is not to say that his wishes must prevail, any more than those of a fully capable patient must prevail. We cannot always have what we want. Nor will it always be possible to ascertain what an incapable patient's wishes are. Even if it is possible to determine what his views were in the past, they might well have changed in the light of the stresses and strains of his current predicament'.[90]

Further important considerations for clinicians arising from this judgment are the legal interpretations of 'futile' and 'recovery'. The Supreme Court indicated that 'futility' should refer only to treatment that would not be effective at all or would offer no benefit to the patient whatsoever. Also, rather than a return to health, 'recovery' should be about 'resuming a quality of life which the patient would regard as worthwhile'.[90] The judgment goes on to endorse the guidance given in the GMC's *Treatment and Care towards the End of Life: Good Practice in Decision-Making*,[91] which should be essential reading for those involved in end-of-life decision-making.

Anorexia nervosa

Anorexia nervosa presents problems both of the assessment of capacity and whether or not patients should be forced to continue with treatment. The three judgments discussed here all relate to cases of severe and unremitting anorexia nervosa. All three patients were deemed (after much deliberation by clinicians and the Court of Protection) to lack capacity to consent to the serious medical treatment at issue. The treatment was recognised as causing considerable distress in all three cases. Ms E's death was imminent, she was refusing to eat, and was taking only a small amount of water.[92] The chance of successful treatment (with 'full recovery') for Ms E was considered to be in the region of 20–30%. The judge held that it was in her best interests to be fed against her wishes. Ms L was described in the judgment as having 'anorexia nervosa of a severity and unremitting nature which is extraordinarily rare in the United Kingdom'.[93] Furthermore, 'Ms L's frail physical condition and compromised liver function means that the likelihood of death if force feeding were to be attempted on a chemically sedated basis would run at close to 100%'. In this case, the judge held that it was lawful not to provide Ms L with nutrition and hydration with which she did not comply and to provide palliative care in the terminal stage of her illness. Ms X suffered from severe and unremitting anorexia nervosa, alcohol dependence and end-stage cirrhosis of the liver.[94] The expert considered that the chance of successful outcome was 5% or less. The judge decided that Ms X should not be compelled to have treatment for her anorexia, but expressed the hope that she would realise the benefit of treatment.

The different legal outcomes – whether or not the court authorised the treatment to continue or stop – were largely determined by whether or not every treatment with a prospect of success had been tried.

'Do not attempt cardiopulmonary resuscitation' (DNACPR) decisions

In a recent court case a family challenged a hospital where a DNACPR order had been put in place without consultation with the patient, who had capacity.[95] The court found that the patient's rights under Article 8 of the ECHR had been violated. This finding has influenced advice in relation to communicating resuscitation decisions in the third edition of *Decisions Relating to Cardiopulmonary Resuscitation*, published by the Resuscitation Council (UK).[96]

A further DNACPR case is that of VT.[97] It provides some insight into how to consider 'burdensome', mentioned earlier, and the status of the family and clinicians. VT was a 73-year-old Muslim man with a history of stroke, insulin-dependent type II diabetes, hypertension, chronic renal impairment and mobility problems. He was cared for at home by his family. He experienced a cardiac arrest at home from which he did not regain consciousness. His family objected to a DNACPR order being placed in his notes. The NHS trust sought a declaration that it would be unlawful to provide intensive care or CPR in the event of a further cardiac arrest.

During the court hearing, an intensive care anaesthetist gave evidence on the experience of a patient who requires intensive care, including the passage and maintenance of cannulas, the experience of intubation, ventilation and weaning, circulatory support and many other unpleasant measures. The family was of the view that this suffering would be the will of Allah and that to withhold CPR or intensive care would not be in VT's best interests as it would deprive him of suffering, which they regarded as a purifying process in preparation for death. The judge believed that VT would have shared this view and the family was correct to expect their view to be taken into account. However, the judge could not allow the family's view to prevail because in allowing VT to suffer, they were expecting the clinical team to harm him for no medical reason or benefit: 'It can hardly be right to expect doctors to cause pain for no justifiable medical reason other than to accommodate the religious or other beliefs of a patient. It would require those who, through medical training and personal beliefs, want to help the patient, to do the exact opposite – that would be neither ethical nor lawful in my judgment'.[97]

In circumstances where a DNACPR order is to be made the patient concerned, where possible, should be involved in the decision unless there is compelling evidence that it would cause psychological or physical harm (not merely distress). If the clinician's opinion is that any attempts at CPR would be futile, they must tell the patient. The patient could then request a second opinion, although if the multidisciplinary team is in agreement with the decision, they have no obligation to arrange this. In the case of incapacitous patients, the Resuscitation Council guidance[96] reinforces that the decision not to resuscitate is a clinical decision, but that clinicians must consult with anyone with substitute decision-making powers, anyone named by the patient as someone to be consulted and anyone engaged in caring for the patient or interested in the patient's welfare. The guidance also emphasises that where consultees are not available immediately, a senior clinician need not delay a DNACPR decision, but must inform the consultees at the earliest opportunity. Where an adult lacks capacity and has no family, friends or other advocate to consult, there is no absolute requirement to consult an Independent Mental Capacity Advocate if it is clear to the medical team that CPR would not restart the patient's heart and breathing for a sustained period. However, if there is genuine doubt about whether CPR would have a realistic chance of success or if the decision is finely balanced, an Independent Mental Capacity Advocate must be involved, or if one is unavailable at the time the decision has to be made, one should be consulted at the earliest opportunity.

Consent in 16- and 17-year-olds has been discussed in Chapter 1 and is also relevant to DNACPR decisions. With some exceptions, the provisions of the MCA apply to young people of this age who lack capacity, and it is generally those with parental responsibility who make decisions on their behalf. Be mindful of the complexity of the law of consent in children and young people.

Practical considerations for clinicians

Although much of the guidance outlined below might seem obvious, and good practice for clinicians, there are plenty of clinical examples where this process has not been applied. Therefore before placing DNACPR on the notes of a patient who lacks capacity (although many of the considerations are the same if capacity is preserved) you must:

► assess and document capacity for each decision
► consult with the multidisciplinary team and document the decision
► involve those close to patient and document views, taking into account cultural and religious factors
► consult an Independent Mental Capacity Advocate if the situation demands it
► review the DNACPR status if the patient's clinical condition changes
► make careful records of best interests discussions
► follow your trust or hospital policy – but don't expect the DNACPR form to provide all the evidence that might be needed in the face of a challenge
► try to define outcomes in clinical terms
► be wary of using words such as 'futility' and 'recovery', especially to justify withholding or withdrawing treatment – these are not narrow clinical definitions and have a 'best interests' component to their use
► explain to the family in detail what you believe the patient is likely to be experiencing in a treatment you consider to be burdensome to the patient
► be careful when using terms such as 'quality of life': this requires a value judgement perhaps better made by those who know the patient best

▶ let relevant others know when you have made a DNACPR decision

▶ be familiar with the GMC's *Treatment and Care towards the End of Life*.[91]

Antipsychotic prescription and dementia

There are, of course, highly relevant and topical issues that commonly affect patients who lack capacity on which there is no clear case law. Prescribing antipsychotics to patients with dementia has not been the subject of a reported Court of Protection case, yet it typifies decision-making under the MCA. Professor Sube Banerjee's report[98] drew attention to the risks associated with the use of antipsychotic drugs in the management of behavioural and psychotic symptoms in dementia. Professor Banerjee estimated that some 180000 people with dementia were being treated with antipsychotic medication each year in the UK and that, of those, only 20% derived some benefit from the treatment. He pointed to the emerging consensus with respect to negative side-effects that are attributable to antipsychotic medication, for instance the increase in cerebrovascular adverse events and death. Furthermore, most atypical antipsychotic drugs appear to have a little impact on levels of disturbance.

We have argued elsewhere[99] that the prescription of antipsychotic medication for people with dementia may fall within the remit of section 37 of the MCA regarding serious medical treatment, i.e. what is proposed is likely to have serious consequences for the patient. 'Serious consequences' are those that could have a serious impact on the patient, either from the effects of the treatment itself or from its wider implications (see Chapter 6). Section 37 requires that, unless the patient has someone to speak for them, an Independent Mental Capacity Advocate must be instructed and consulted. Notwithstanding this, to ensure that medical treatment for behavioural and psychotic symptoms in dementia is in a patient's best interests, and therefore lawful, prescribers are advised to observe a framework of assessment, consultation, prescribing and review. It is relatively easy to fall foul of these requirements in an area where opinions among clinicians and carers can be highly polarised in either direction.

CHAPTER 9

The Mental Health Act

The existence of the Mental Health Act means that the rules and procedures for the non-consensual admission to, and treatment in, hospital for mental disorder are different from those for physical illness. As a judge has said 'In our judgment Parliament provided an exhaustive code concerning compulsory admission to hospital in Part II MHA. Sections 2–6 cover procedure for hospital admission which include in s.4 admission in emergency situations. We do not accept that there is any lacuna in MHA in relation to the period when a person is at the hospital pending an application under s.2 or s.4 MHA': neither the MCA nor the 'common law principle of necessity' applies.[24]

The single most important difference between the Mental Health Act and the Mental Capacity Act is that the MHA authorises compulsory admission to and detention in hospital, and medical treatment despite the patient's capacitous refusal. In other words, most of the rules and principles you've just read about don't necessarily apply if the person has a mental disorder that presents risks to their health or safety or to other people. A very brief overview of the grounds for detention and treatment is given below. For those who may need to use the MHA there are many helpful texts.[1,14,100,101]

► The key message is: consider the MHA when faced with a patient with a mental disorder who, in your opinion, requires treatment that the patient is refusing or that cannot be given for some other legal reason (e.g. because there is a valid, applicable advance refusal or refusal by the donee of a lasting power of attorney).

The essential difference between the two Acts was demonstrated in the sad case of a 26-year-old woman who took her own life by swallowing anti-freeze.[102] That she had the capacity to refuse treatment, and did so refuse, was confirmed by all the health professionals who saw her. It is much less clear whether any consideration was given to detaining and treating her under the Mental Health Act, which, in the circumstances, may well have been an option.

It should be noted that there are some small differences between the English and Welsh Mental Health Acts and significant differences between their Codes of Practice. Quotes in this text are from the English version of the Codes of Practice (there are two Codes of Practice relating to the MHA, one for England[14] and the other for Wales[101]).

Least restrictive option and maximising independence

Where it is possible to treat a patient safely and lawfully without detaining them under the Act, the patient should not be detained. Wherever possible a patient's independence should be encouraged and supported, with a focus on promoting recovery.

Empowerment and involvement

Patients should be fully involved in decisions about care, support and treatment. The views of families, carers and others, if appropriate, should be fully considered when taking decisions. Where decisions are taken that are contradictory to views expressed, professionals should explain the reasons for this.

Respect and dignity

Patients, their families and carers should be treated with respect and dignity and listened to by professionals.

Purpose and effectiveness

Decisions about care and treatment should be appropriate to the patient, they should have clear therapeutic aims, promote recovery and be performed to current national guidelines and/or current best practice guidelines.

Efficiency and equity

Providers, commissioners and other relevant organisations should work together to ensure that the commissioning and provision of mental healthcare services are of high quality and are given equal priority to physical health and social care services. All relevant services should work together to facilitate timely, safe and supportive discharge from detention.

Criteria for detention

These vary a little between the sections and, in simple terms, are all self-evident. The person must suffer from, or appear to suffer from, a mental disorder (or the MHA would not be relevant), that disorder must cause some sort of risk for the person or other people (or there's no need to intervene), the risk can't be assessed or managed without the person being in hospital (a person cannot be detained in hospital if they don't need to be in hospital) and the person isn't agreeing to the admission (or they wouldn't need detaining).

Please note that we are referring here to detention in hospital – detention does not include Community Treatment Orders or guardianship.

What counts as appropriate (medical) treatment in differing circumstances and for different conditions will probably be clarified by the courts over time. At the time of writing, there have been a number of cases that have all said the same thing. It is agreed that appropriate treatment is more than just locking a person up, but in none of the cases was it decided that appropriate treatment was not being provided. Although the threshold is low, there hasn't yet been a case in which the court decided that appropriate treatment was not being provided.

The detention criteria are as follows.

For assessment (section 2)

Mental disorder of a nature or degree that warrants the patient's detention in hospital for assessment.

For treatment (section 3)

Mental disorder of a nature or degree that makes it appropriate for the patient to receive medical treatment in hospital, and appropriate treatment is available.

Note

Although one is called an assessment order and the other a treatment order, the authority to force treatment on patients is the same for both sections.

In an emergency (section 4)

Urgent necessity for the patient to be detained under section 2 and waiting to complete section 2 would cause an undesirable delay.

If the patient is already an in-patient (section 5(2))

The Registered Medical Practitioner (or Approved Clinician) in charge or their Nominated Deputy believes that an application under Part 2 (a section 2 or 3) ought to be made. The Registered Medical Practitioner is the consultant responsible for the care of the patient and may be from any specialty. This section can only be used if the patient is already admitted. It cannot be used, therefore, in the accident and emergency department.

Mentally disordered persons found in public places (section 136)

This section enables a police officer to remove to a 'place of safety' someone they find in a place to which the public has access who appears to be suffering from mental disorder and to be in immediate need of care or control. This would include accident and emergency departments. A patient can be moved between one place of safety and another within the overall time limit (72 hours).

Warrant to search for and remove patients (section 135)

This is for the same purpose as a section 136 but for a person who is in private premises. It permits an Approved Mental Health Professional to obtain a warrant authorising a police officer to enter premises where there is reasonable cause to suspect that a person believed to be suffering from mental disorder:

▶ has been, or is being, ill-treated, neglected or kept otherwise than under proper control, in any place within the jurisdiction of the justice, or

▶ is living alone in such a place and is unable to care for themselves.

A warrant may also be obtained authorising a police officer to enter premises to 'take or retake' a patient who is already detained under the MHA.

Notes

▶ The preferred place of safety, unless the patient is too violent or physically ill, is a dedicated place (often called a 136 suite) within a mental health service. Police stations and accident and emergency departments may be used as places of safety (but only if the patient is too disturbed to move or is in need of medical treatment respectively).

▶ Patients may also be subject to compulsion through Guardianship Orders or Community Treatment Orders.[1]

Terminology

Mental disorder

Mental disorder is defined in the MHA as 'any disorder or disability of the mind', a very broad definition. Affective, schizophrenic and delusional, neurotic, stress-related and somatoform (such as anxiety, phobias, obsessive–compulsive), post-traumatic and hypochondriacal disorders are included. So are organic, personality and eating disorders, mental and behavioural disorders caused by psychoactive substance use, non-organic sleep and sexual disorders, autism spectrum disorders, and behavioural and emotional disorders in children and adolescents. The MHA Codes of Practice[14,101] give further guidance.

The definition of mental disorder has two caveats.

▶ First, dependency on alcohol or drugs is excluded from the definition, so patients cannot be detained if they suffer solely from such dependency.

Other conditions relating to alcohol or drug misuse, such as intoxication or withdrawal, are not excluded. Nor are patients excluded if they suffer from such dependency and another mental disorder.

▶ Second, people with a learning disability ('a state of arrested or incomplete development of the mind which includes significant impairment of intelligence and social functioning') and no (other) mental disorder can be detained on a treatment order, only if the disability is associated with abnormally aggressive or seriously irresponsible behaviour. (This caveat does not apply for sections 2 and 4.)

Nature or degree

To explain the difference one can do no better than quote the judge in *R v Mental Health Review Tribunal for the South Thames Region ex parte Smith*:[103]

'Although the wording of this phrase is disjunctive ['or' not 'and'] the nature and degree of the patient's mental disorder will be inevitably bound up so that it matters not whether the issue is dealt with under nature or degree. The word 'nature' refers to the particular mental disorder from which the patient suffers, its chronicity, its prognosis and the patient's previous response to receiving treatment for the disorder [the judge rejected the view that 'nature' is static] and the word 'degree' refers to the current manifestation of the patient's disorder.'

Health or safety or protection of other persons

This should be self-explanatory but seems to be misunderstood. It is quite different from the often-expressed grounds for detaining someone under the MHA, i.e. dangerousness. It is perfectly proper and lawful to detain a patient solely because 'it is necessary for his health'.

In hospital

This bit is more important than may at first be apparent. A patient cannot be detained under the MHA unless they need to be in hospital. That is why, when completing the documentation, the clinician has to say why other interventions (e.g. in the community) won't be adequate to achieve the necessary assessment or treatment. 'In hospital' is also important in relation to section 17 leave of absence.

It is surprising how often there are arguments over what a hospital is. Section 145 MHA defines 'hospital' so that it includes 'any health service hospital within the meaning of the National Health Service Act 2006', which in turn includes 'any institution for the reception and treatment of persons suffering from illness' and any 'clinics, dispensaries and out-patient departments maintained in connection with any such [...] institution'.

Appropriate medical treatment is available

This criterion applies only to treatment orders, e.g. sections 3 or 37. It is explained in the MHA as follows:

'references to appropriate medical treatment, in relation to a person suffering from mental disorder, are references to medical treatment which is appropriate in his case, taking into account the nature and degree of the mental disorder and all other circumstances of his case'.

The MHA Codes of Practice clarify this in a number of ways:

▶ the appropriate medical treatment test is met even if the treatment is not the ideal treatment; nor does it need to address every aspect of the patient's condition

▶ appropriate medical treatment is available even if the patient refuses to accept it

▶ in some cases, the ward milieu may be sufficient to meet the available appropriate medical treatment test.

Medical treatment

This term is much broader than would be expected from general usage. It includes 'nursing, psychological intervention and specialist mental health habilitation [learning new skills], rehabilitation [relearning lost skills] and care'. Furthermore, the MHA allows the detention of a person for the receipt of appropriate treatment only if 'the purpose [of the treatment] is to alleviate, or prevent a worsening of, the disorder or one or more of its symptoms or manifestations'.

Does there have to be a clear evidence base for this 'purpose' test to be met or can it rest on the personal view of the doctor making the section 3 recommendation? Suppose the patient has failed to respond to the treatment in the past: can a doctor still maintain that the purpose of the intervention is to alleviate or prevent a worsening? If the patient's condition continues to deteriorate despite treatment, does this mean that the 'purpose' test should fail? These are questions that we have been asked. Although it is true that exactly what is meant by 'purpose' isn't clear, it seems to us that such questions should be answered in the same way as clinicians have always decided whether or not to recommend a medical intervention for a patient. These are clinical decisions.

Who is required

Section 2 – Admission for assessment

Two Registered Medical Practitioners – one section 12 approved, the other with previous knowledge of the patient if practicable – and an applicant (Approved Mental Health Professional or Nearest Relative).

Section 3 – Admission for treatment

Two Registered Medical Practitioners – one section 12 approved, the other with previous knowledge of the patient if practicable – and an applicant (Approved Mental Health Professional or Nearest Relative). The Nearest Relative must not object to the application (positive agreement is not required).

Section 4 – Admission for assessment in cases of emergency

One Registered Medical Practitioner and an applicant (Approved Mental Health Professional or Nearest Relative).

Section 5(2) – Application in respect of patient already in hospital

The Registered Medical Practitioner or Approved Clinician in charge of the patient or their Nominated Deputy.

Use of the Mental Health Act in a general hospital

The MHA makes no distinction between 'mental health/psychiatric' and 'general' hospitals. They are all just hospitals. In practice, however, there may be several major differences.

Most general hospitals do not employ Approved Clinicians and cannot therefore appoint a Responsible Clinician. If general hospitals are to detain patients, i.e. be the detaining authority, there must be some arrangement, such as a service-level agreement, to enable Approved Clinicians from a local mental health hospital to be appointed as Responsible Clinicians within the general hospital. Patients cannot be transferred to a general hospital under section 19 (Regulations as to transfer of patients) unless a Responsible Clinician can be appointed. This does not stop transfer under section 17, i.e. on leave of absence.

The general hospital will also require MHA 'Hospital Managers' and administrators. We are aware of arrangements whereby the services of mental health trust personnel are used for these purposes.

More difficult is where general hospitals aren't registered with the Care Quality Commission to take detained patients. It is important to note that it is unlawful to use section 5(2) in these hospitals because there are no Hospital Managers to whom the 5(2) report can be 'furnished'.

The process

It doesn't matter who starts the process (general practitioner, hospital consultant, psychiatrist, nurse, social worker, relative, etc.). The patient, for sections 2 and 3 (the most common), must be examined by two Registered Medical Practitioners, who make and date medical recommendations, on or before the date the Approved Mental Health Professional makes an application. The Codes of Practice require the Registered Medical Practitioners to make a 'direct personal examination of the patient and their mental state'. If neither Registered Medical Practitioner has previous knowledge of the patient – previous attendance at, for example, a case conference about the patient would count as 'previous knowledge' – then it is recommended that both Registered Medical Practitioners should be section 12 approved.

There must be no more than 5 days between the two medical examinations. The days on which the medical examinations are made aren't counted. So if the first medical recommendation is made on a Monday, the second must be made on or before the following Sunday. If the two Registered Medical Practitioners examine the patient at the same time, they may, if they wish, make a joint recommendation on the appropriate form (although we wouldn't advise this because the medical recommendations on a joint form can't be amended if faulty). Otherwise they must each make separate recommendations. The Approved Mental Health Professional then has 14 days from the second medical examination in which to make an application (for section 4 the application must be made within 24 hours).

Both Codes of Practice state that it is the responsibility of the 'doctor' to find a bed. This will be on behalf of the hospital. Most hospitals have 'bed managers' of one sort or another. This also means that the Registered Medical Practitioner has to think about the type of bed (acute, psychiatric intensive care, medium secure, etc.) required. All other responsibilities lie with the Approved Mental Health Professional. These include identifying and consulting the Nearest Relative (although if a Registered Medical Practitioner knows the Nearest Relative then preliminary discussion would be helpful), transporting the patient to hospital, making sure children and pets are properly cared for and ensuring that the patient's home is secure. The Codes recommend using the ambulance service, with police support if necessary, to ensure safety.

Note

Specialist skills or facilities may be needed to undertake assessment of particular patients. Children, those who don't have English as a first language, patients with severe learning disability or deafness, or those who present particular risks are examples. Clinicians should not undertake assessments for which they do not have the necessary training or experience. This does not mean that they should walk away – they should, of course, help identify an appropriate person or service and assist with the urgent needs of the patient in the meantime.

Section 2 or section 3?

The MHA Codes of Practice give guidance on whether section 2 or section 3 is most appropriate. The Code for England says that section 2 should only be used if:

► the full extent of the nature and degree of a patient's condition is unclear

► there is a need to carry out an initial in-patient assessment in order to formulate a treatment plan, or to reach a judgement about whether the patient will accept treatment on a voluntary basis following admission, or

- there is a need to carry out a new in-patient assessment in order to re-formulate a treatment plan, or to reach a judgement about whether the patient will accept treatment on a voluntary basis.

Section 3 should be used if the patient is already on a section 2 or if:

- the nature and current degree of the patient's mental disorder, the essential elements of the treatment plan to be followed and the likelihood of the patient accepting treatment as an informal patient are already sufficiently established to make it unnecessary to undertake a new assessment under section 2.

The Code for Wales is similar.

It should be noted that the patient's Nearest Relative can prevent application of a section 3 by objecting to it. However, it is considered improper to use a section 2 rather than section 3 simply because the Nearest Relative might object. The Code for England states that:

> 'Consultation must not be avoided purely because it is thought that the nearest relative might object to the application [...] If the nearest relative objects to an application being made for admission for treatment under section 3, the application cannot be made. If it is thought necessary to proceed with the application to ensure the patient's safety and the nearest relative cannot be persuaded to agree, the AMHP will need to consider applying to the county court for the nearest relative's displacement under section 29 of the Act.'

The Welsh Code is stronger.

Additional points

- The usual team of two Registered Medical Practitioners and an Approved Mental Health Professional must not have defined conflicts of interest for personal (e.g. they are first-degree relatives), professional (e.g. in the same team or one directs the other) or business reasons (e.g. business partners). The full list for England and Wales is in their Codes of Practice. Although the information is given in the Codes of Practice, it is taken from Statutory Instruments and is therefore law rather than guidance.
- If the choice is between a section 4, avoiding all conflicts of interest, or a section 2 or 3 but all three assessors work in the same team, then a section 2 or 3 is the preferred option (England only).
- If the application is for detention in an independent (fee-paying) hospital, then (in England) only one of the Registered Medical Practitioners may be employed by that hospital (in Wales neither may be employed by the independent hospital).
- Although an Approved Mental Health Professional is the preferred applicant, an application can be made by the patient's Nearest Relative.
- Patients can be moved, using the authority of the MHA, between hospitals only if they are detained by reason of an application. Section 4 patients, like sections 2 and 3, have an applicant. Patients held under section 5(2) do not have an applicant.

- Section 5(4) is known as the nurse's holding power. A nurse 'of the prescribed class' (a qualified mental health or learning disability nurse) can detain for up to 6 hours a patient who is 'receiving treatment for mental disorder as an in-patient'. This is to hold the patient until a section 5(2) can be applied.
- In section 5(2), what is an in-patient? The MHA Code of Practice defines it as 'a person who is receiving in-patient treatment in a hospital'. This excludes out-patients and those receiving treatment in an accident and emergency department. In one case, the judge said that the word 'suggests the allocation and use of a hospital bed'.[104]
- The authority to transport the patient to hospital under sections 2, 3 or 4 comes from the application (which, in turn, is founded on the medical recommendation(s)).
- Hospitals are not required to accept patients. The patient is formally detained in hospital only when the papers are accepted by the Hospital Managers (in practice, this is usually a nurse on the ward, the MHA administrator or medical records staff, on behalf of the Hospital Managers).

The key points of this chapter thus far are summarised in Table 9.1 (pp. 118–119).

Treatment under the MHA

The authority to give medical treatment to a patient who is detained or subject to a Community Treatment Order under the MHA comes from Part IV of the Act – 'Consent to treatment'. If the patient is informal, or under a section to which Part IV does not apply, or the treatment is for a physical illness unrelated to the mental disorder, then the same rules apply as explained in the rest of this book – capacitous consent or the MCA.

Part IV is subdivided into:

- Part 4 [sic] – detained patients
- Part 4A – Community Treatment Order patients (unless they have been recalled to hospital).

The following relates to Part 4 – detained patients. Community Treatment Order patients cannot be treated compulsorily. If it is necessary to give a CTO patient treatment against their wishes, then the patient must first be recalled to hospital (and so become subject to Part 4 of the MHA).

- **Which patients are not subject to Part 4?**
  All detained patients are subject to Part 4 except patients detained under the very short sections – sections 4, 5(2), 5(4), 35, 135, 136 – and certain 'forensic' sections – sections 37(4), 45A(5), 73 or 74 not recalled to hospital.

It is important to recognise that Part 4 either applies to a particular detention section or it does not. There is no detention order to which

Table 9.1 Key information governing the detention and treatment of patients under Part II and sections 135 or 136 of the Mental Health Act

	Section 2	Section 3	Section 4	Section 5(2)	Section 135	Section 136
By whom?	Section 12 approved RMP plus another RMP plus an AMHP or NR. One RMP should have previous knowledge of the patient if practicable	Section 12 approved RMP plus another RMP plus an AMHP or NR. One RMP should have previous knowledge of the patient if practicable	RMP plus AMHP or NR	AC or RMP in charge of the patient, or their ND	Magistrate plus AMHP (and PC and RMP)	PC
Where?	Patient anywhere	Patient anywhere	Patient anywhere	Patient an in-patient in hospital (*not* in an A&E department)	Patient in premises specified in the warrant	Patient in a place to which public have access (not person's own home), including A&E department
For how long?	28 days	6 months	72 hours	72 hours	72 hours	72 hours
First criterion	Mental disorder	Mental disorder	Urgent necessity for the patient to be detained under section 2	RMP/AC/ND believes that an application under Part II (section 2 or 3) should be made	Mental disorder	Mental disorder
Second criterion	Disorder of a nature or degree that warrants the detention of the patient in hospital	Disorder of a nature or degree that makes it appropriate for the patient to receive medical treatment in hospital	Waiting to complete section 2 would cause an undesirable delay		The person is ill-treated, neglected, 'kept other than under proper control' or unable to care for themselves	Person is in immediate need of care or control

(continued)

Table 9.1 *Continued*

	Section 2	Section 3	Section 4	Section 5(2)	Section 135	Section 136
First purpose	Hospital detention for assessment (followed by treatment)	Medical treatment in hospital				
Second purpose (and also a criterion)	In the interests of the patient's health or safety or for the protection of other persons	It is necessary for the patient's health or safety or for the protection of other persons				In the interests of the person or for the protection of other persons
Final criterion			Appropriate treatment is available		To be taken to a place of safety	To be taken to a place of safety
Medical treatment for mental disorder authorised by MHA?	Yes	Yes	No	No	No	No
Right of appeal?	To Tribunal within first 14 days	To Tribunal once in any renewal period	No right of appeal	No right of appeal	No right of appeal	No right of appeal
Renewable?	No	Yes	No	Yes	No	No
Progression to CTO?	No	Yes	No	No	No	No
Authority to move patient without being cancelled[a]	Yes	Yes	Yes	No	From one place of safety to another	From one place of safety to another

AC, Approved Clinician; A&E, accident and emergency department; AMHP, Approved Mental Health Professional; CTO, Community Treatment Order; ND, Nominated Deputy; NR, Nearest Relative; PC, Police Constable; RMP, Registered Medical Practitioner.

a. Can the section be used as the authority to move the patient from one hospital to another without it being cancelled?

Part 4 partially applies. That is why, despite gossip to the contrary, there is no difference between section 2 and section 3 in relation to consent to treatment: Part 4 applies to both sections.

Medical treatment for mental disorder

Medical treatment for mental disorder includes treatment that is for the causes or consequences of the mental disorder. Therefore, a clinician can treat, without the patient's consent, a physical illness that is causing a mental disorder. A commonly asked question is whether or not self-harm resulting from mental disorder can be treated without consent. For example, may acetylcysteine be given to a detained patient who has taken an overdose of paracetamol? The answer is yes. The judgment also includes medical investigations that are required in order to give the patient medication for treating mental disorder (e.g. blood tests may be carried out if lithium or clozapine are prescribed). It is important to note that the patient must be detained under a section to which Part 4 of the MHA applies (e.g. section 2 or 3) and the 'physical' treatment must be for the cause or consequence of the mental disorder.

Treatment for physical illness unrelated to mental disorder

Mr C was a patient in a high secure hospital who developed gangrene of his leg secondary to chronic diabetes.[105] The surgeon advised that the patient would die if his leg was not amputated. The patient, who believed himself to be a doctor of international eminence (this was a delusion), refused surgery, saying he had complete confidence that God and the hospital staff would save him. He accepted that it was possible he would die from the gangrene but remained adamant he did not want surgery. The case went to the High Court. The judge said that the physical disorder, the gangrene, was unrelated to the patient's mental disorder and the patient's refusal was not part of, or related to, his psychotic thinking and therefore the MHA was not relevant. Furthermore, the patient was able to understand, remember, believe and weigh the information in the balance in order to make a decision and express that decision (although the case pre-dated the MCA, the rules relating to incapacity were almost identical to current rules, except that 'believe' has been removed as it was thought to be unnecessary – it is subsumed within 'weigh in the balance'). The patient was deemed to have capacity to make the decision and refused the surgery. He, and his leg, recovered.

Caesarean section without consent

Two cases[106,107] in which the MHA was used to force a Caesarean section on women who, for different reasons, refused to consent are important. These are not to be confused with the often-quoted case of the woman who consented to a Caesarean section but refused at the last moment because she had a 'needle phobia':[108] the MHA was not relevant in that case.

One of the cases[106] concerned a woman with schizophrenia detained under section 3. The High Court decided that the Caesarean section was 'ancillary' to the treatment of her mental disorder because:

▶ it would prevent a deterioration in the patient's mental state

▶ for the successful treatment of the patient's schizophrenia it was necessary for her to give birth to a live child

▶ the administration of antipsychotic drugs had been necessarily interrupted by pregnancy and could not be resumed until the child was born.

The Caesarean section was lawful under section 63 of the MHA.

To explain the marked contrast in the decision in this case from that in the case of Mr C,[105] the judge said that 'Treatment of C's gangrene was not likely to affect his mental condition'.

In the other case,[107] a woman with pre-eclampsia who refused a Caesarean section was detained under the MHA for assessment of her mental state. A High Court authorisation for the Caesarean section was then sought and obtained, and the procedure was carried out. A subsequent Court of Appeal said that the patient had been unlawfully detained. Although she may have had a mental disorder, this was clearly not the reason for her detention because she was neither assessed nor treated for her mental disorder. The judicial authority for the Caesarean section had been based on false and incomplete information. The Court repeated that a competent pregnant woman can refuse treatment even if that refusal may result in harm to her or her unborn child, i.e. the unborn child does not have a legal existence other than as part of its mother.

There is no golden rule that says that any intervention can or can't be made using the authority of Part IV of the MHA. The circumstances of the particular case will determine the lawfulness or otherwise.

The only applicable general rule is: if in doubt, seek guidance from a senior colleague or a lawyer.

Medical investigations without consent

The courts have ruled that there is no difference between investigations into and treatment of mental disorder. A doctor had sought the High Court's permission to undertake computerised tomography of a patient (with schizophrenia and a suspected brain tumour) who refused. The judge said that there is 'no distinction between diagnostic and therapeutic procedures.[109] The same criterion governs their lawfulness'.

Treatment groups under the MHA

There are five different groups of treatments under the MHA:

1 treatments that always require both the patient's capacitous consent and a statutory second opinion (section 57); the rules for this group of interventions apply to informal patients as well as detained ones;

2   treatments that always require either capacitous consent or a statutory second opinion and which cannot be given in the face of capacitous refusal (except in an emergency) (section 58A);

3   treatments that can be given on the authority of the Responsible Clinician (or, when appropriate, Approved Clinician in charge of that treatment) for 3 months and then require capacitous consent or a statutory second opinion (section 58);

4   treatments that can always be given on the authority of the Responsible Clinician (or, when appropriate, Approved Clinician in charge of that treatment) (section 63);

5   emergency ('urgent') treatments (section 62).

The Secretary of State for Health has the authority to add, or remove, treatments from each category as they think appropriate. The surgical implantation of hormones for the purpose of reducing male sex drive was added to the first category (section 57) in this way. There has been a great deal of discussion as to whether or not forced tube-feeding for mental disorder (anorexia nervosa) should be added to group 3 (section 58). To date this has not been done.

Section 62 Urgent treatment

Compliance with sections 58 (medication for mental disorder) and 58A (electroconvulsive therapy) is not required if the treatment meets the description of 'urgent treatment'. 'Urgent treatment' can be authorised by any Registered Medical Practitioner or an Approved Clinician who is a nurse prescriber. There are four categories of 'urgent treatment' (only the first two apply to section 58A electroconvulsive therapy). 'Urgent treatment' is treatment that is:

▶   immediately necessary to save a patient's life, or

▶   immediately necessary (and not irreversible) to save a serious deterioration in the patient's condition, or

▶   immediately necessary (and neither irreversible nor hazardous) to alleviate serious suffering, or

▶   immediately necessary (and neither irreversible nor hazardous) and the minimum interference required to prevent the patient from behaving violently or being a danger to themselves or others.

What is meant by irreversible and hazardous isn't made entirely clear even though they are defined: 'For the purposes of this section treatment is irreversible if it has unfavourable irreversible physical or psychological consequences and hazardous if it entails significant physical hazard'.

In addition, if a capacitous patient has been consenting to medication and then withdraws their consent, they may be required to continue with the medication if stopping it 'would cause serious suffering to the patient'.

Section 63 Treatment not requiring consent

This section applies to treatments that can always be given on the authority of the Responsible Clinician (or Approved Clinician in charge of that treatment) and for which the patient's consent is not required (this does not mean that consent shouldn't, if possible, be sought). These include any medical treatment not covered by section 57 or 58 (including 58A) above. It covers not only nursing, psychological treatments, and so on, but also medication for mental disorder for the first 3 months (section 58 applies only after 3 months).

Placebo medication (for mental disorder)

Can patients subject to the MHA be given placebo medication for their mental disorder? One dictionary definition of placebo is 'a substance given to someone who is told that it is a particular medicine [...]' (Cambridge Dictionaries Online: http://dictionary.cambridge.org), another 'a substance that is administered as a drug but has no medicinal content [...]' (Chambers: http://www.chambersharrap.co.uk).

One side of the argument says that a placebo isn't medication. If this is the case, section 58 is irrelevant, and the placebo is treatment under section 63, which doesn't require the patient's consent (although the Code of Practice says that 'the patient's consent should still be sought'[14]). The alternative point of view is that it is medication as far as the patient is concerned. This means it needs to be discussed properly with the patient in order to determine whether or not the patient is capacitous and consenting – which is obviously self-defeating.

Covert medication (for mental disorder)

Unlike a placebo, covert medication is medication. Its use, therefore, is subject to section 63 for the first 3 months and section 58 thereafter. It is again difficult to see how one can assess whether or not the patient is capacitous and consenting without discussing the medication with them. There is an additional difficulty with covert medication. A patient whose condition improves as a result of covert medication will presume that they have got better without medication. Should the patient appeal against their section to a Tribunal (or Hospital Managers) they would be in an impossible position. They would, entirely reasonably, argue that they didn't need medication. The Responsible Clinician would have to explain why this wasn't true. The Upper Tribunal has established that this information (that the patient is being given covert medication) cannot be withheld from the patient if they have made a Tribunal appeal.[110]

123

References

1   Zigmond T (2014) *A Clinician's Brief Guide to the Mental Health Act* (3nd edn). RCPsych Publications.

2   Department for Constitutional Affairs (2007) *Mental Capacity Act 2005: Code of Practice.* TSO (The Stationery Office).

3   Ministry of Justice (2008) *Mental Capacity Act 2005: Deprivation of Liberty Safeguards. Code of Practice to Supplement the Main Mental Capacity Act.* TSO (The Stationery Office).

4   *Re F (Sterilisation: Mental Patient)* [1989] 2 FLR 376.

5   *Savage v South Essex Partnership NHS Foundation Trust* [2010] EWHC 865 (QB).

6   *Re A (Children) (Conjoined Twins)* [2000] 4 All ER 961.

7   *Rabone v Pennine Care NHS Foundation Trust* (2012) UKSC 2, (2012) MHLO 6.

8   *Herczegfalvy v Austria (A/242-B)* (1993) 15 EHRR 437.

9   *Wilkinson, R (on the application of) v Broadmoor Hospital, Responsible Medical Officer & Ors* [2001] EWCA Civ 1545.

10 *MS v The United Kingdom 24527/08* [2012] ECHR 804.

11 *Winterwerp v The Netherlands* (1979) 2 EHRR 387.

12 *R (G) v Nottinghamshire Healthcare NHS Trust* [2008] EWHC 1096.

13 *Storck v Germany 61603/00* (2005) ECHR 406.

14 Department of Health (2015) *Code of Practice: Mental Health Act 1983: Presented to Parliament Pursuant to Section 118 of the Mental Health Act 1983.* TSO (The Stationery Office).

15 *Re T (Adult: Refusal of Treatment)* [1992] 3 WLR 782, [1993] Fam 95.

16 *Re B (Adult: Refusal of Medical Treatment)* [2002] 2 All ER 449.

17 *Heart of England NHS Foundation Trust v JB* [2014] EWHC 342 (COP).

18 *Bolam v Friern Hospital Management Committee* [1957] 1 WLR 582.

19 *Bolitho v City & Hackney Health Authority* [1997] 3 WLR 1151.

20 *Pearce v United Bristol Healthcare NHS Trust* [1999] PIQR P59.

21 General Medical Council (2008) *Consent Guidance: Patients and Doctors Making Decisions Together.* GMC.

22 *Re W (A Minor) (Medical Treatment)* [1992] 4 All ER 627.

23 *ZH (by his Litigation Friend) v Metropolitan Police Commissioner* [2012] All ER (D) 134 (Mar).

24 *R (Sessay) v South London and Maudsley NHS Foundation Trust* (2011) EWHC 2617 (QB).

25 Department of Health, National Institute for Mental Health in England (2009) *The Legal Aspects of the Care and Treatment of Children and Young People with Mental Disorder: A Guide for Professionals.* National Institute for Mental Health in England.

26 General Medical Council (2012) *0–18 Years: Guidance for all Doctors.* GMC.

27 General Medical Council (2012) *Consent Guidance: Involving Children and Young People in Making Decisions*. GMC.

28 *An NHS Foundation Hospital v P* (2014) EWHC 1650 (Fam), (2014) MHLO 35.

29 House of Lords (2013) *Mental Capacity Act 2005 Select Committee: Oral and Written Evidence – Volume 1 (A – K)*. TSO (The Stationery Office) (http://www.parliament.uk/documents/Mental-Capacity-Act-2005/mental-capacity-act-2005-vol1.pdf).

30 House of Lords (2013) *Mental Capacity Act 2005 Select Committee: Oral and Written Evidence – Volume 2 (L–W)*. TSO (The Stationery Office) (http://www.parliament.uk/documents/lords-committees/mental-capacity-act/mental-capacity-act-2005-vol2.pdf).

31 Select Committee on the Mental Capacity Act 2005 (2014) *Mental Capacity Act 2005: Post-Legislative Scrutiny*. TSO (The Stationery Office) (http://www.publications.parliament.uk/pa/ld201314/ldselect/ldmentalcap/139/139.pdf).

32 *B v Croydon Health Authority* (1995) Fam 133.

33 *Nottinghamshire Healthcare NHS Trust v RC* [2014] EWCOP 1317.

34 Ministry of Justice (2008) *Mental Capacity Act 2005: Deprivation of Liberty Safeguards. Code of Practice to Supplement the Main Mental Capacity Act*. TSO (The Stationery Office).

35 *DCC v KH* (2009) COP 11729380.

36 Okai D, Owen G, McGuire H, *et al* (2007) Mental capacity in psychiatric patients: systematic review. *British Journal of Psychiatry*, **191**: 291–297.

37 Raymont V, Bingley W, Buchanan A, *et al* (2004) Prevalence of mental incapacity in medical inpatients and associated risk factors: cross-sectional study. *Lancet*, **364**: 1421–1427.

38 Law Commission (1995) *Mental Incapacity*. TSO (The Stationery Office).

39 *PC and NC v City of York Council* [2013] EWCA Civ 478.

40 Mahoney FL, Barthel DW (1965) Functional evaluation: the Barthel Index. *Maryland State Medical Journal*, **14**: 61–65.

41 Nasreddine ZS, Phillips NA, Bédirian V, *et al* (2005) The Montreal Cognitive Assessment (MoCA): a brief screening tool for mild cognitive impairment. *Journal of the American Geriatrics Society*, **53**: 695–699.

42 Neuroscience Research Australia (2012) *The Addenbrooke's Cognitive Examination: ACE-III*. Neuroscience Research Australia.

43 Brown PF, Tulloch AD, Mackenzie C, *et al* (2013) Assessments of mental capacity in psychiatric inpatients: a retrospective cohort study. *BMC Psychiatry*, **13**: 115.

44 Cairns R, Maddock C, Buchanan A, *et al* (2005) Reliability of mental capacity assessments in psychiatric in-patients. *British Journal of Psychiatry*, **187**: 372–378.

45 Marson DC, McInturff B, Hawkins L, *et al* (1997) Consistency of physician judgments of capacity to consent in mild Alzheimer's disease. *Journal of the American Geriatrics Society*, **45**: 453–457.

46 *CC v KK* [2012] EWHC 2136 (COP), (2012) MHLO 89.

47 *Re F (Mental Health Sterilisation)* [1990] 2 AC 1.

48 Joyce T (2007) *Best Interests: Guidance on Determining the Best Interests of Adults Who Lack the Capacity to Make a Decision (or Decisions) for Themselves [England and Wales]*. British Psychological Society.

49 Butler-Cole V, Ruck Keene A (2010) *Preparing Care Plans, Transition Plans and Best Interests Assessments for Court of Protection Proceedings*. Thirty Nine Essex Street.

50 *Cardiff Council v Peggy Ross* (2011) COP 28 October, 12063905.

51 *Re K, Re F* [1988] 1 All ER 358.

52 *Wychavon District Council v EM (HB)* [2011] UKUT 144 (AAC).

53   Lee S (2007) *Making Decisions: The Independent Mental Capacity Advocate (IMCA) Service. Helping People Who are Unable to Make Some Decisions for Themselves* (OPG606, 2nd edn). Office of the Public Guardian.

54   Department of Health (2010) *The Third Year of the Independent Mental Capacity Advocacy (IMCA) Service 2009/10*. Department of Health.

55   Department of Health (2005) *Research Governance Framework for Health and Social Care* (2nd edn). Department of Health.

56   *Statutory Instruments 2006 No. 2810: Mental Capacity Act 2005 (Appropriate Body) (England) Regulations 2006*. TSO (The Stationery Office).

57   *HL v United Kingdom* [2004] 40 EHRR 761.

58   Cairns R, Brown P, Grant-Peterkin H, *et al* (2011) Judgements about deprivation of liberty made by various professionals: comparison study. *Psychiatrist*, **35**: 344–349.

59   *Cheshire West and Chester Council v P* [2014] UKSC 19, (2014) MHLO 16.

60   *JE v DE and Surrey County Council* [2006] EWHC 3459 (Fam).

61   *Re MIG and MEG* [2010] EWHC 785 (Fam).

62   *Re P and Q; P and Q v Surrey County Council; sub nom Re MIG and MEG* (2011) EWCA Civ 190.

63   *Cheshire West and Chester Council v P* [2011] EWHC 1330 (COP).

64   *Cheshire West and Chester Council v P* [2011] EWCA Civ 1257.

65   McNicholl A (2014) Half of Deprivation of Liberty Safeguards cases breaching legal timescales. Community Care (http://www.communitycare.co.uk/2014/10/01/50-deprivation-liberty-safeguards-cases-breaching-legal-timescales). Accessed 2 April 2015.

66   Association of Directors of Adult Social Service (2014) Number of DoLS referrals rise tenfold since Supreme Court ruling (Friday 6 June). ADASS (http://www.adass.org.uk/number-of-dols-referrals-rise-tenfold-since-supreme-court-ruling-jun-14). Accessed 2 April 2015.

67   *NHS Trust & Ors v FG* [2014] EWCOP 30.

68   *Rochdale MBC v KW* [2014] EWCOP 45.

69   *Statutory Instruments 2008 No. 1858: The Mental Capacity (Deprivation of Liberty: Standard Authorisations, Assessments and Ordinary Residence) Regulations 2008*. TSO (The Stationery Office).

70   *A NHS Trust v Dr A* [2013] EWCOP 2442.

71   *Hillingdon v Steven Neary* [2011] EWHC 1377 (COP).

72   Chief Coroner (2013) *Chief Coroner's Guidance No. 16: Deprivation of Liberty Safeguards (DoLS)*. TSO (The Stationery Office). (http://www.judiciary.gov.uk/wp-content/uploads/2013/10/guidance-no16-dols.pdf).

73   *Re X and others (Deprivation of Liberty)* [2014] EWCOP 25.

74   *Re X and others (Deprivation of Liberty)* [2014] EWCOP 37.

75   Ministry of Justice (2012) *Judicial and Court Statistics 2011*. Ministry of Justice.

76   *Statutory Instruments 2007 No. 1744 (L. 12) Mental Capacity, England and Wales: The Court of Protection Rules 2007*. TSO (The Stationery Office).

77   Howard R, Hendy S (2004) The sterilisation of women with learning disabilities – some points for consideration. *British Journal of Developmental Disabilities*, **50**: 133–141.

78   Newman M (2014) *Rape has been 'decriminalised' for the most vulnerable says senior Met adviser*. Bureau of Investigative Journalism (https://www.thebureauinvestigates.com/2014/02/28/rape-has-been-decriminalised-for-the-most-vulnerable-says-senior-met-adviser).

79   *X City Council v MB, NB and MAB* [2006] 2 FLR 168.

80   *MM v Local Authority X* [2007] EWHC 2003 Fam.

81   *R v C* [2009] 1 WLR 1786.

82   *D County Council v LS* [2010] EWHC 1544.

83   *D Borough Council v AB* [2011] EWHC 101.

84   *A Local Authority v H* [2012] EWHC 49.

85   *A Local Authority v TZ* [2013] EWHC 2322 (COP) .

86   *IM v LM and Others* [2014] EWCA Civ 37.

87   *Re Y (Mental Incapacity: Bone Marrow Transplant)* [1996] 2 FLR 787.

88   *Airedale NHS Trust v Bland* [1993] AC 789 HL.

89   *Re CW; A Primary Care Trust v CW* [2010] EWHC 3448 (COP).

90   *Aintree University Hospitals NHS Foundation Trust v David James* [2013] UKSC 67, (2013) MHLO 95.

91   General Medical Council (201) *Treatment and Care towards the End of Life: Good Practice in Decision Making.* GMC.

92   *Re E (Medical treatment: Anorexia)* [2012] EWHC 1639 (COP), (2012) MHLO 55.

93   *Re L; The NHS Trust v L* [2012] EWHC 2741 (COP), (2012) MHLO 159.

94   *An NHS Foundation Trust v Ms X* [2014] EWCOP 35, (2014) MHLO 96.

95   *R (Tracey) v Cambridge University Hospital NHS Foundation* [2012] EWHC 3670 (Admin), (2012) MHLO 146.

96   (2014) *Decisions Relating to Cardiopulmonary Resuscitation: Guidance from the British Medical Association, the Resuscitation Council (UK) and the Royal College of Nursing* (3rd edn). Resuscitation Council (UK).

97   *An NHS Foundation Trust v VT and A* [2013] EWHC B26 (Fam).

98   Banerjee S (2009) *The Use of Antipsychotic Medication for People with Dementia: Time for Action. A Report for the Minister of State for Care Services.* Department of Health.

99   Branton T, Brindle N, Zigmond A (2009) Antipsychotic treatment for dementia may now constitute 'serious medical treatment' under the Mental Capacity Act 2005. *BMJ*, **339**: b4818.

100   Department of Health (2008) *Reference Guide to the Mental Health Act 1983.* TSO (The Stationery Office).

101   Welsh Assembly Government (2008) *Mental Health Act 1983: Code of Practice for Wales.* TSO (The Stationery Office).

102   BBC News (2009) Doctors 'forced' to allow suicide. 1 Oct. BBC (http://news.bbc.co.uk/1/hi/england/norfolk/8284728.stm).

103   *R v Mental Health Review Tribunal for the South Thames Region ex parte Smith* [1998] EWHC 832.

104   *R (on the application of DR) v Mersey Care NHS Trust* [2002] EWHC 1810.

105   *Re C (Adult, refusal of treatment)* [1994] 1 All ER 819.

106   *Tameside & Glossop Acute Services Unit v CH (a patient)* [1996] 1 FLR 762.

107   *St George's Healthcare NHS Trust v S; R v Collins and others, ex parte S* [1998] 3 All ER 673.

108   *Re MB (Medical Treatment)* [1997] 2 FLR 426.

109   *Re H (Mental Patients: Diagnosis)* (1992) FLR Jul 1; [1993] 1: 28–33.

110   *RM v St Andrew's Healthcare* [2010] UKUT 119 (AAC), HM/0837/2010.

Index

Compiled by Linda English